SERPENT OF THE NILE

To My Mother

SERPENT OF THE NILE

Women and Dance in the Arab World

Wendy Buonaventura

INTERLINK BOOKS
An Imprint of Interlink Publishing Group, Inc.
NEW YORK

First American paperback edition published 1994 by

INTERLINK BOOKS
An imprint of Interlink Publishing Group, Inc.
99 Seventh Avenue
Brooklyn, New York 11215

Library of Congress Cataloging-in-Publication Data

Buonaventura, Wendy, 1950-
    Serpent of the Nile: women and dance in the Arab
world/by Wendy Buonaventura.
        p.   cm.
    Bibliography: p.
    Includes index.
    ISBN 1-56656-117-5
    1. Dancing--Arab countries = History.   2. Women
dancers--Middle East--History.   3. Women
dancers--Egypt--History. I. Title.
GV1704.B86   1994
793.3'1953082--dc20   89-15393
                                          CIP

Designers: Andréa Saba - Ariane Couteau.
Printed and bound in France by Lescure-Théol.

Contents

Acknowledgements

I am indebted to many people who have helped me in the preparation of this book. Among them I would like to thank the following: Amel Benhassine-Miller, for her contribution on North African dance; Maggie Caffrey for her thought-provoking comments on the manuscript; Hossam Ramzy for his musical expertise; Ibrahim Farrah, who generously allowed me to make free use of the *Arabesque* picture collection in New York; the staff of the Victoria and Albert Museum in London, who helped me track down many unknown paintings; Badr al-Haj and Nadim Shehadi, for their considerable contribution to the illustrations; and Mai Ghoussoub and André Gaspard of Saqi Books, who gave me the opportunity to realize a long-term project in this book. Most of all I would like to thank Nick Campion, who contributed his historical expertise, and who has encouraged and supported me in more ways than I can say.

Glossary

almeh (pl. *awalim*). Woman well-versed in the arts, especially music and poetry

baksheesh. Tip, gratuity

bendir. North African sieve-like hand drum covered in goatskin

bezima. Silver clasp used to attach front and back sides of a dress at the shoulders

caliph. Temporal and spiritual head of Islam

cengi. Turkish dancer

chikhat. Moroccan dancer

daff. Egyptian sieve-like hand drum covered in fish skin

daholla. Large *tabla*

darabouka. North African goblet-shaped hand drum covered in fish skin

felucca. Single-sailed boat

galabiya. Loose, floor-length robe

ghaziya (pl. *ghawazee*). Egyptian dancer, originally from gypsy tribe

haik. Length of cloth draped around the body to make a dress; North African

hammam. Steam bath

kanoon. Stringed instrument, the predecessor of the harp and piano

khawal. Boy dancer who imitates the women's dance

khediva. Wife of *khedive* (ruler of Egypt from 1867 to 1914 governing as a viceroy of the Sultan of Turkey)

Maghreb. Morocco, Tunisia and Algeria

maqam (pl. *maqamat*). Scale in Arabic music

mashrabiya. Ornamental wooden 'windows'

mazhar. Very large tambourine

mouled. Popular religious festival to celebrate the birth of the Prophet Muhammad

mukhannath. 'Effeminate', a title given to male musicians who replaced women after the latter's seclusion in the harem

mutrube. Persian dancer/courtesan

nai. Arabic flute made of bamboo

oud. Arabic lute

rababa. Predecessor of the violin, with a coconut-shell body

raks al-baladi. Dance of the people, the traditional form of the women's solo dance

raks al-hawanem. Dance of the ladies

raks al-sharqi. Dance of the East

reque. Egyptian tambourine

souq. Market

tabl baladi. Very large drum, processional musical instrument hung around the neck

tabla. Goblet-shaped hand drum, made of earthenware or metal, open at one end, covered at the other with fish skin

tagine. North African stew of meat and vegetables

taqsim (pl. *taqasim*). Musical improvisation, generally on a solo instrument, or with one instrument prominent

tar. North African tambourine

tarboosh. Type of red pillbox hat formerly popular in Egypt and Turkey

zhagareet. Ululation: cry of encouragement or approval made by women, often in response to a gifted dancer

Introduction

*Beside the fire, as the wood burns black, A laughing dancer in veils of light,
Whose dance transforms the darkness to gold.*

Abu Abd Allah ben Abi-l-Khisal

Time stands still in remote places. Traditions are slow to change and memory is long. By the banks of the Nile, not far from Aswan, we moored our boat, a single-sailed *felucca*, and two of our company went ashore to buy food. It was nearly dusk. A flight of crumbling steps led steeply down to the bank, and at the sight of our boat a horde of children in white *galabiyas* appeared and came running down to take a closer look at us. 'Tourists!' they shrieked, pointing at two of the men in the boat who were wearing shorts. These poor tourists with their bare, reddened legs had evidently forgotten to put their clothes on. The children laughed and, with mocking faces, mimed the clicking of cameras. A woman was fetching water from the river, scooping it into an enormous earthenware pot. She rolled up a length of cloth to rest the pot on. Then, with a single deft movement, she lifted the pot and rested it carefully on her head. Balancing it with one hand she turned away and, catching up her skirt with the other, began climbing to the top of the steps. I was struck by how gracefully she moved, despite the heavy weight she was carrying, her hips swaying from side to side as she picked her way barefoot over the uneven ground and disappeared from view.

As the sky began to grow dark the children started to drift away. One of them, a little girl in a *galabiya* which reached like a nightgown almost down to her ankles, had been standing there all the while, staring at us. A tiny figure with a tangle of dark hair, she could not have been more than 5 or 6 years old.

9

Learning the dance in the south of Egypt. Late 19th century. Tinted photograph. Private collection

Suddenly she came to life and began dancing, rolling her hips and saucily shaking her bottom at us. Raising her arms above her head, she imperiously snapped her fingers, her face full of glee, while some of the other children clapped out a rhythm for her. Then she came down to the bottom of the steps and held out her hand for money. But our boatman shoo'ed her away, and as we pushed out again into the middle of the river, he called out to the children as they stood and watched us go, teasing them with their own words, 'Tourist! Camera! *Baksheesh!*'

Every day that I had spent in Egypt there had been sudden, unexpected glimpses of dancing. Once it was two young girls with scarves round their hips, seen through the open window of a house in the middle of the afternoon, dancing together to music from the radio. Another time it was a group of gypsies on an open patch of ground outside the *souq*. It is easy to find dancing in Egypt, for in most of the Arab-Islamic world dance still has a role to play in everyday life. It has not become a thing apart, as it has in the West.

For some years I had been teaching and performing Arabic dance, in particular the traditional women's solo in its Egyptian form, *raks al-baladi* (dance of the people). Variations of this type of dance, and the hybrid it has produced, *raks al-sharqi* (dance of the East), are found all over North Africa and the Middle East. No dance has exerted a more powerful fascination, nor been described in greater detail by passing strangers.

My own experience of Egyptian *baladi* goes back some twelve years. The first time I saw it, it struck me as something rare and magical. I thought then, and still think, that it is the most eloquent of female dances, with its haunting lyricism, its fire, its endlessly shifting kaleidoscope of sensual movement.

Today's dance is a far cry from its ancient ancestor, one of the oldest dances in creation, yet traces of its distant past still cling to it and often reveal themselves in unexpected ways. It was once found throughout the world, a dance in which movement of the hips — sometimes vigorous, sometimes soft and sinuous — was the principal expression. Originally it had a precise meaning in terms of ritual and ceremony, for it expressed the mysteries of life and death as people understood them then.

Like all early dance, it was originally connected with religious worship, at a time when religion was an integral part of daily life and had relevance to every aspect of human existence. But as primitive cultures grew more sophisticated and civilization suppressed the faiths of a former age, so too were the rituals connected with these bygone religions suppressed. Thus the female pelvic dance died out in many parts of the world. In some areas, however, it turned from a religious rite into a secular entertainment.

Accounts of it have come down to us from all over the world and from all periods of history. An ancient Greek version had, as its essential characteristic, the rotation of the hips and abdomen. In Cadiz in the first century AD dancers performed 'sinking down with quivering thighs to the floor'.[1] In the seventh century AD a Persian scholar, describing the chief attributes of a great dancer, pointed out 'a marked agility in twirling and swaying the hips'.[2] Chief among the areas where this type of dance survived is today's Arab-Islamic world. There, an art developed out of the old rite which became, in time, a dance of great richness and subtlety.

When dance ceased to be merely a means of self-expression and a part of communal ceremony and became a secular entertainment, it was taken up and refined by the professional performers who now emerged on the scene. With this transition, a line was drawn between the acceptable and unacceptable faces of this dance of the hips, which was a bold, sensual form of expression and sometimes a highly erotic one. In the Arab world, as in patriarchal cultures the world over, its acceptability or unacceptability was intimately bound up with the role of women in society and with what was permitted and what was forbidden them.

On the acceptable side was dance as a social pastime, performed in the home by women to entertain each other. On the unacceptable side was professional dance, which was the province of

Alex Bida. *Egyptian dancer.* c.1860. Watercolour. Victoria & Albert Museum, London

gypsies, minority communities and the poorer members of society. They were distrusted for their free and easy ways, their reputation for dishonesty (like that of entertainers in general), and their refusal to accept the social mores of the community at large. However much professional dancers were welcomed into the home to animate family festivities, dancing in front of strangers was not considered an acceptable activity for respectable women.

The story of how Egyptian *baladi* and its equivalent in other Arab-Islamic countries changed from a private to a professional entertainment, how it was exported to the West and became, on the one hand, a subject of scandal and, on the other, an enduring inspiration for Western art is the main subject of this book. It is the story of how an ancient art has survived against the odds.

In its own society, Arabic dance has rarely been the subject of study and representation in the arts. Most records of it, whether written or visual, are the work of Western artists and travellers, in particular from the nineteenth century, the 'Orientalist' age. We are indebted to the Orientalists for the record they have bequeathed to us, for without them we would have no detailed knowledge of Arabic dance in former times. Arabic poetry gives us only an occasional glimpse of it — and not the

A party in the harem. 18th century. Aquatint. Private collection

Persian musician.
Qajar dynasty,
early 19th century.
Oil painting.
Victoria & Albert
Museum, London

dance itself, but the transforming effect of its beauty on the eye of the beholder, the way it intoxicates the senses and creates a timeless rapture of the spirit. In general, however, appreciations of this dance are rarely found in Arabic literature.

Islamic society has never quite resolved its ambivalence towards female dancers, who, in many respects, defy its laws concerning the conduct of women in society. A faith in which the sacred and the secular are indissolubly linked, Islam is the corner-stone of existence for the majority of people in the Arab world. Certain verses in the Quran forbidding idolatry encouraged the growth of an artistic tradition in which no natural object could serve as a symbol of the divine. This proscription on naturalistic representation has helped shape an artistic tradition which is primarily abstract and stylized.

Interestingly enough, while the women's dance has often been frowned upon in its own society, it has none the less developed a form which harmonizes closely with the visual arts of Islam, especially regarding its effect on the onlooker. It is a dance which soothes the mind rather than distracts it. Its hypnotic quality, which provokes an inner calm in the spectator, is one element which has often fascinated outside observers:

> Hours pass and it is difficult to tear oneself away. This is the way the motions of the dancing girls affect the senses. There is no variety or vivacity, and seldom is there a variation through any sudden movement, but the rhythmic wheeling exhales a delightful torpor upon the soul, like an almost hypnotic intoxication.[3]

These words of nineteenth-century French novelist Charles Gobineau were echoed by many others who witnessed the dance in the nineteenth century, a time when interest in the Orient, as it was then known, was at its height. Many painters and writers travelled to the Arab world at that time, in search of inspiration for their work.

Women were the most popular subject of Orientalist art. The dancers were the main attraction

Previous page:
Otto Pilny. *Desert dance*. Mid-19th century. Oil painting. Sotheby's, London

for travellers who, even though their reasons for visiting the Arab world were many and varied, never refused the opportunity of going to see the famous dancing girls. Indeed, many travellers actively, even obsessively, sought them out. The result was that they became the symbol of a sensuality which, in the eyes of the outside world, characterized Oriental life. They were also a forbidden attraction and thus had a particular allure. In former times the most skilled among the dancers had enjoyed great prestige and been respected for their knowledge and artistry. But by the nineteenth century their status had dropped and they were widely regarded as disreputable. Travellers who went looking for them out of idle curiosity stayed to marvel at their artistry none the less. Women as well as men were enthralled by *baladi*, which was at first regarded merely as 'a curious and wonderful gymnastic'.[4] Later it came to be admired for its skill and the subtle nature of its eroticism.

A dance in the ruins of Karnak. Late 19th century. Engraving

An American journalist named G.W. Curtis went to Egypt in the middle of the nineteenth century. The dancers had been exiled from Cairo since 1834 (see ch.3) and Curtis travelled 500 miles up the Nile to the little town of Esna to find the most celebrated dancer of her day, Kutchuk Hanem. He ends his long description of the entertainment he enjoyed at her house with the comment, 'It was a lyric of love which words cannot tell. Profound, Oriental, intense and terrible.'[5]

From the middle of the nineteenth century onwards dancers from the Arab world began arriving in the West to appear at the great trade fairs which were designed to display the new technological achievements of the era, as well as to exhibit different aspects of world culture. From the public's point of view, the entertainment was the biggest attraction of these exhibitions. Mock-ups of Algerian coffee-houses, Egyptian theatres and Persian palaces with their indigenous entertainers attracted a good deal of press comment, which tended to highlight what delicate Victorian sensibilities considered the 'shocking' aspect of the dance. The result was that people flocked to see it, thus confirming its notoriety.

Facing page:
Syrian musician. 1890. Photograph.
Private collection

Bonfils. *Group of musicians and dancers.* 1885. Tinted photograph.
Private collection

The nineteenth century was a time of upheaval for the West, due in large part to the gr of industrialism. While bankers and busines were looking into the dawn of the technologica artists were looking back nostalgically at an an way of life not yet ruined by the cre mechanization of the developing world. A hand pioneering women who were moulding We dance into new forms found their greatest inspi in the philosophy and arts of the East.

In the first two decades of the twentieth century, dance was the most influential of the arts. The strong Oriental influence on the new, developing forms of dance filtered down through its sister arts. Stage design, fashion, theatre, book illustration and the decorative arts were all influenced by the Western perception of the Arab-Islamic world. The many 'exotic interpreters' and 'shimmy specialists', as they were called, did little more than move about in a vaguely undulatory fashion, clad in multi-coloured veils which they later proceeded to discard.

It was a fantasy of the East, a fantasy of 'Oriental' dance. Even serious performers found no technical inspiration in Arabic dance, though they none the less presented their offerings as authentic dances of the East. Occasionally a performer attempted to present genuine work based on the spirit of the East, as she understood it. The American dancer Ruth St Denis, in whose work a spiritual or religious element was paramount, is one example. Yet she was in a minority. As for Arab performers who had come to Europe and America in search of work, they were greatly influenced by Western dance and from the beginning of the twentieth century outside elements began creeping into their repertoire. A dancer's small company of musicians grew into a full-scale orchestra which came to include a number of Western instruments. *Baladi* had previously been enriched by the dance of Persia, Turkey and India, with which it shared certain ways of using the body. European dance was based on a completely different technique and use of performance space.

From this period onwards, *baladi* began to undergo a series of fundamental changes. Like all art forms taken out of their cultural context and offered up commercially, it lost something of its essential spirit as well as its integrity of form. In the past it had been performed more or less on the spot, an intensely concentrated, almost meditative art. Now performers twirled about the floor, went up on the balls of their feet, even wore ballet pumps and high-heeled shoes in deference to European aesthetics. Their dress gave way to a Hollywood-inspired costume which expressed nothing so much as current Western notions of glamour, and Arabic dance thus moved into the world of cabaret.

The nightclub act which resulted can, when performed by dancers of skill and artistic integrity, be appreciated on its own terms. Performed, as it often is today, by unskilled dancers of all nationalities who have little or no expertise, this 'belly dance' is now treated with derision in the West. It is a far cry from the dance which still lives on in the Middle East and North Africa, performed by women in the privacy of the home. Yet it is still the best-known manifestation of Arabic dance in the West.

Today, however, a new direction is being taken by a growing number of Arab and Western dancers who are pioneering the theatrical development of Arabic dance. They are taking traditional *baladi*, *sharqi* and bedouin dance and developing them in a theatrical context where the art can be seen and appreciated at its best.

As a social activity in the Arab world, this dance has retained its intimate nature and many of the customs surrounding it. It is still handed down from mother to daughter and performed by women for their own entertainment. It is still performed in the open air for money thrown by the crowd, as well as in the homes of the wealthy, where performers are richly rewarded. And it remains an essential ingredient of any occasion when communities gather to enjoy themselves, especially for important celebrations such as weddings.

In Aswan one night I was taken to a wedding some way out of town. We drove along bumpy, unlit roads and when it became too difficult to navigate, we left our car and continued on foot. We stumbled through the darkness over piles of rubble, guided by the distant sound of drumming and voices raised

French author Colette in an Oriental fantasy during her brief career in music hall. c.1908. Tinted photograph

Facing page, top:
Lekegian. *Dancers from the East.* c.1880. Photograph. Private collection

Facing page, bottom:
Turkish entertainer. c.1890. Tinted photograph. Private collection

in song. Turning a corner, we found ourselves in the midst of the wedding party. Men and women were celebrating at opposite ends of the narrow street, bounded by high walls. The women had gathered in a little group in front of where the bride and groom were sitting on a raised platform in the embrasure of the wall.

A woman in green and gold, wearing a sequinned scarf over her hair, was dancing surrounded by her friends. I guessed her to be in her late thirties. Her face was thin and lined, yet her dark eyes burned with pleasure, and the movement of her hips, pumping up and down and this way and that, seemed to shoot out sparks, creating an electric current all around her. Catching my eye, she drew me into the circle to accompany her. When the other women saw that I knew their dance they pressed in closer, delighted. All around me I heard the shrill echo of the *zhagareet*, or ululation, that trilling of the tongue ending in a high-pitched cry which signifies approval. One by one the others took it in turns to dance with the woman in green and she matched her movements to theirs, sometimes, to their great amusement, subtly mocking them, sometimes launching into a duet, sharing a joke in the shrug of a shoulder, a mutual secret in the flick of a hip. How about that?, her hips, more eloquent than words, seemed to say.

When we went to have some refreshment in the courtyard she showed me her seven children, ranging in age from a baby to an adolescent. Seeing her up close, under the bare light bulbs strung between the trees, I noticed for the first time the marks which a hard life had left on her face, etched around her eyes and across her forehead. One of her daughters brought me a glass of sweetened, chilled hibiscus tea and we sat and chatted in sign language, with the occasional English and Arabic word thrown in for good measure.

By the time I left, the dancing had begun again. I turned round at the corner of the street and saw that the woman in green was on her feet once more. She danced on for her own pleasure, moving in the old spirit of a dance whose flame neither commercialism, religious disapproval nor changing times have managed to extinguish.

Facing page:
Muhammad Racim. *Two Algerian women dancing together beneath a single veil*. c.1830. Miniature

Demetre Chiparus. *Sunburst.* c. 1930.
Bronze and ivory statue. Christie's,
London

ANCIENT ECHOES

I am the child of the earth and the starry skies.

Orphic inscription

All dance comes from life, and in particular from our need to express ourselves and make sense of our existence. By its very nature it is one of the most powerful means of auto-intoxication we have, developing energy in the body and then releasing it. Its *raison d'être* is reflected in the origins of our word for it, which has a similar derivation in languages the world over. 'Dance' comes from the Sanskrit *tanha*, meaning 'joy of life', while the Arabic *raks* and the Turkish *rakkase* both derive from the Assyrian *rakadu*, meaning 'to celebrate'.

Dance satisfies many other needs besides that of celebration, for it helps us discharge the pent-up energies of everyday life and reinforces our identity as part of the social group. It has always been therapeutic, or healing, and has traditionally been a way of attracting a partner. Yet only in tribal communities and remote areas does it retain its old application of sympathetic magic, as a ritual device used to encourage both human fertility and the growth of crops.

All dance was once part of religious ritual, and in some cultures it still is. In early times religion was a part of everyday life, with all natural occurrences touched by it. The rising and setting of the sun each day, the cycles of the harvest, and the birth and death of the body were all seen as the result of powerful, mysterious forces beyond conscious understanding. People learnt to deal with them first through the creation of a spirit world and then through myth and its attendant rituals, whose power lay in their ability to illuminate the unknown without reducing it to the mundane.

Spirits were everywhere: under stones, in trees, in the air; indeed, in many remote areas, belief in a spirit world is as strong today as it has ever been. In Egypt in the not too distant past, people believed that the spirits or 'genii' of the fire had to be placated with the words 'Pardon O genii' whenever something was thrown into the flames. Meanwhile, in Britain

Thomas Fuller. *'Dancing maidens',
ancient Greece*. 1650. Engraving

Druids continue to worship the spirits of trees and annually enact a sacred rite at Stonehenge to usher in the summer.

In prehistoric times our forebears served nature rather than the reverse, which was to happen as civilizations grew more sophisticated. Socio-political structures subsequently evolved in which people worshipped the priestesses and priests, kings and god-kings who came to assume the power of nature. In the ancient world, before human beings regarded themselves as the supreme expression of creation, they were content with a more humble role in the natural order. And so as to maintain this order they devised rituals which involved making offerings to the spirits to please them. Sympathetic magic was used to shape events and their outcome in every sphere of existence, including hunting, where it was believed that an animal's behaviour could be influenced by imitating its movements.

Before the invention of language the main vehicle of self-expression was the body. However, as language developed and grew increasingly complex, mankind's deepening sensibility made it possible to deal in abstractions, with the result that language came to replace bodily movement as the principal means of communication. Yet there are some things which cannot be communicated through speech; they can only be expressed through the language of the body.

Dance had a central role to play in ancient ritual, and over the years grew to embody the value systems of the cultures which shaped it. As life grew more sophisticated, the mystic, tribal acts of early communities gave way to organized religious ceremonies, the most important of which were those concerned with the fertility of the earth and the human race. A detailed examination of the fascinating web of ritual and belief which patterned our ancestors' lives is outside the scope of the present book; certain elements must nevertheless be mentioned briefly, for they have a bearing on our subject.

In all rites of passage, men and women have traditionally been separated. This custom still obtains in some parts of the world, especially among tribal peoples and those living in remote areas, and is an unconscious vestige of our pagan past, which has to do with the sacred nature of the event. In certain countries of the Arab-Islamic world today, the separation of men and women is observed not only in human rites of passage such as weddings, but in everyday life, where women live and conduct their household affairs in separate quarters from the men.

Among the ancient rites connected with fertility are the initiation rituals of puberty, where sexual education for girls is relayed via erotic singing and dancing. The initiation ceremony of the African Kuta[6] takes place in and near water. The young girls and women wade into a river in which a hut of branches and leaves has been constructed, crouching down so that only their heads remain above water. At a certain moment in the ceremony one of the older women emerges from the river, tears off her loincloth and performs a 'most salacious' dance. The young girls then enter the hut for their initiation, which culminates in 'a number of dances, one of

South Sea dancers. 1770s.
Copperplate engraving

which symbolizes the sexual act'. The Kuta is only one of many tribes who use erotic song and dance in their rituals of puberty, a tradition which is by no means confined to the African continent. In cultures such as these, all male puberty rites consist of men pretending to take on women's powers and imitating their actions.[7]

Moving on to the next important fertility rite we find rituals designed to attract a partner and celebrate marriage. Erotic pelvic dancing has always played an important part in the long-drawn-out ceremonies used by tribal communities for sexual bonding. Although it is impossible to know the exact form a dance took in ancient times, our knowledge of sympathetic magic, in which imitative movement was thought to influence natural occurrences, can provide a clue, as can intuition and the work of anthropologists who have studied the practices of tribal communities still in existence.

In the *World History of the Dance*[8] Curt Sachs

Tahitian dancers entertaining the queen. 1770s. Copperplate engraving

describes a pelvic dance of the Bafioti in Loango, West Africa. This dance had a part to play in ancestor worship and the glorification of future generations via the birth process. A similar dance has been found in the South Seas, New Guinea, the Solomon Islands, eastern Polynesia and throughout Africa. Joseph Spurrier, writing about the Hawaiian *hula*,[9] describes its aim as 'the attraction of the gods and the stimulation of their procreative powers, exactly after the manner of the stimulation of man'. Performed in a grass skirt resting on the hips, to the accompaniment of rousing, joyous music, the *hula* is one of the most graceful of these pelvic dances. Its principal movement is a vigorous, accelerating rotation of the pelvis, interspersed with a side-to-side swinging of the hips.

In ancient Greece there existed a number of fertility dances based on pelvic rotation, swaying of the hips and an exaggerated shaking of the bottom. Lillian B. Lawler[10] groups together several of them, all named after wooden cooking utensils, dances in which 'the characteristic motion is a rhythmical and voluptuous rotation of the hips, suggestive of "stirring" or "grinding" '. One was known as the *igdis* or 'grinding mortar' dance. In another, 'the performer rotated the hips and jerked the body in a manner reminiscent of the motion of a pestle being used to grind food in a mortar'. Coupled with this dance was a movement which translates as 'writhing, twisting, as a willow wand'. The ancient Greek writer Pollux linked together all these dances, which he characterized by their 'swaying rotation of the hips'. In *The Metamorphosis* by Apuleius, a girl stirring a pot on the fire attracts a young man's attention by the rhythmic swaying of her hips and shoulders. Lawler comments that all these dances were 'in essence the same thing — stimulating or fertility dances, the exact equivalents being found from primitive times in the ritual of many nature deities'.

The basic link between copulation and conception was made very early on in human history. Various artworks from prehistoric times attest to the fact that men recognized that they had a role to play in the creation of life, although the precise nature of this role was probably unclear to them. To take only one example, there is a stone plaque which was found at a shrine in Catal Huyuk, Anatolia (south-east Turkey), dating back roughly 8,000 years; on one side this plaque shows two lovers embracing, and on the other we find a woman holding a baby.

Fertility rituals not infrequently ended in copulation, which was regarded as a sacred aspect of life in that it ensured the continuation of the human race. Today's climate is very different from those times, when human beings had an understanding of sexual energy untainted by a sense of sin and guilt. These came as a later development of civilization, along with male-centred religions and patriarchy.[11]

In ancient times human fertility was believed to be linked with that of the earth. Our ancestors created myths through which such mysteries became accessible to them, stories imbued with a poetic ambiguity. Throughout the world, myths that are similar in essence have come down to us through the years and can still be found today in children's fairy tales.

Early communities had a vivid, poetic understanding of life, and in time conjured up not only nature spirits but a multiplicity of male and female deities who were regarded as responsible for the natural order. Many ethnologists believe that the earliest and most important of these deities was female. The suggestion that a mother, rather than a father figure was originally worshipped is supported by numerous anthropological studies, though the subject is still one of considerable debate. Goddess figurines thousands of years old have been discovered in many parts of the world, and in the Middle East — the cradle of goddess worship and the area where this faith had its most fervent and persistent support — these statues of female figures have been found dating back approximately 70,000 years before Christ. The earliest works of art ever discovered, they are figures of large-hipped, full-breasted women with their arms aloft as if they were dancing.

Belief in a prime female creator was no doubt shaped by the obvious fact that it was women who gave birth. Women were also assumed to have a magical power which affected the growth of crops, and it is thought that it was women who invented agriculture, which developed roughly simultaneously in many parts of the world. Yet some societies,

Fertility deity from Kushan. 5th century. Red sandstone. Private collection

among them the American Indians, rejected agriculture outright:

> You ask me to dig in the earth? Am I to take a knife and plunge it into the breast of my mother? But then, when I die, she will not gather me again into her bosom. You tell me to dig up and take away the stones. Must I mutilate her flesh so as to get at her bones? Then I can never enter into her body and be born again.[12]

These words, spoken by a prophet of the American Indian Umatilla tribe less than a hundred years ago, reflect a primordial belief linking women with the earth they tilled. It was universally thought that babies were born of the earth; that they came from caves and grottoes, swamps and streams, and that when a woman passed by certain of these places, the spirit of a child entered her body. Reflections of this belief can be found in the ancient Roman term for bastard ('son of the earth'), as well as the Romanian equivalent which means 'child of flowers'.

The idea that woman's magical powers of creation extended to the natural world and that she had a part to play in assisting the growth of crops gave rise to the myth of a Great Mother, or goddess, who was both revered and feared for her mysterious powers. Thousands of years ago, on the hilltops of central Anatolia and the Mediterranean, women enacted dance rites in honour of this goddess, rites from which men were excluded, as they were from all women's ceremonies concerned with fertility.

From the late fourth century BC down to the Christian era many of the most popular female deities in the Hellenistic and Graeco-Roman world came from the East, in particular Syria and Turkey. In Cyprus, birthplace of Aphrodite, the Greek goddess of love and fertility, women performed what have been described as erotic, ecstatic dances, to the accompaniment of wild singing and drumming. The trance, or ecstatic element, was crucial, for it released an energy in the body which helped the dancer enter into another realm of experience and unite with the deity, whose power was thus transferred to her.

From earliest times in the Middle East, women

Hellenistic bronze from Alexandria.
Early 2nd century. Metropolitan
Museum of Art, New York

31

worshipped a female creator under her various guises by having sexual relations with strangers. This custom became formalized in Babylon in the fifth century BC, where every woman undertook to wait at the temple of Mylitta until a man came by and threw her a coin as an invitation to sexual intercourse, an invitation made invoking the name of the goddess. Once this had happened the woman was free to return home and resume her everyday life. Payment was not made to the woman herself, but was an offering to the goddess in return for the man being allowed to take part in her rites. This tradition was current throughout Mesopotamia (Iraq, Kuwait, Turkey, Syria and parts of Iran) and was also found in Egypt, Arabia and Phoenicia (Lebanon).

In Egypt, where the goddesses Hathor and Bastet were worshipped for their powers of fertility, large numbers of women attended their festivals, where they sang and danced and offered themselves to men in the service of the deity. At Hierapolis (Baalbek) in Lebanon, a similar custom was observed in the service of the goddess Attar. The main purpose of all these rituals was to bring the fertilizing power of the goddess into contact with the lives of human beings. In addition, as Hesiod, one of the earliest Greek poets, wrote,[13] the 'sensual magic' of the women helped 'mellow the behaviour of men', and in this way transformed animal instinct into love.

Scholars sometimes refer to a temple priestess whose functions include sexual rites as a *hierodule* (from the Greek, meaning 'sacred servant'). Yet they most often use the term 'sacred prostitute', an unhelpful name in that, to the modern mind, 'sacred' (suggesting dedication to a divine spirit) and 'prostitute' (suggesting defilement) would appear to be contradictory. Our loss of an instinctive life and our division of matter and spirit make it difficult for us to appreciate the ancient belief that sexuality was an integral aspect of spirituality.

Music and dance were found at all celebrations held in honour of fertility deities. The second-century historian Pausanius tells us that in classical Greece temple priestesses performed a dance known as the *kordax*, which involved a rotation of the hips while the feet were held closely together. The *devadassis* (temple priestesses) of India performed voluptuous dances which served 'to promote the joys of fecundity and sex and were featured often [in sculptures] on the outer enclosures of temples'. These beautiful sculptures can be seen today: full-breasted, plump-thighed figures with a girdle tied round their hips and an enigmatic smile on their faces. In the thirteenth century AD 20,000 of these *devadassis* were attached to temples in India, and as late as the end of the nineteenth century they could still be found, though their numbers were greatly diminished by then. Worshippers brought them offerings of flowers, fruit, scented water and costly cloth and ornaments:

> Of all their arts, dancing is the most highly cultivated... consisting of a pantomime made up of the most graceful and alluring dramatic action, gestures, twistings and marvellous undulatory and expressive motions of the torso.[14]

The question that remains is what happened to religious fertility dances as civilizations changed and the old faiths were ousted, often brutally, to make way for the new. Today the majority of the human race follow male-dominated religions and live in patriarchal societies where women's power has been drastically curtailed. It was the ancient Semites who first set about dethroning the old female-centred, or pagan faiths. Unlike other Middle Eastern peoples, the Hebrew tribes allowed no priestesses to take part in their religion. Yet the suppression of paganism and the consequent change in women's status did not happen overnight. It took a long time for the ancient esteem in which women were held to give way to the fear and distrust which have since expressed themselves, throughout the world, in the curtailing of female sexuality and women's place in public life.

There are various theories as to how and why these changes occurred. One is that when man began to understand his role in the creation of life he mistakenly believed that he alone was responsible, and that woman was merely a vessel for his creation. Thus a change from matrileny to patrileny took place; the laws governing women's rights were altered, and men were given absolute authority over the

Dancing yakshi from North India. 16th century. Red sandstone. Private collection

family. In this way women lost their freedom to inherit and pass on property and themselves became possessions, first of their fathers and then of their husbands. The new laws devised to control women's freedom were severe in the extreme and have still not entirely disappeared. An ancient Hebrew custom of condemning a woman to death if she were not chaste at the time of her marriage is still sometimes found today in parts of the Mediterranean and the Arab world.

It took hundreds of years to suppress the goddess faith (and thus the power of women), and throughout this time women continued to worship their old deities in secret, as is revealed in the Old Testament. Vestiges of the goddess faith can still be found in religions the world over, among them Christianity, with its worship of the Virgin Mary, and Islam, whose most sacred emblem, the Kaaba, symbolizes the ancient goddess of Arabia.[15]

Over hundreds of years the old deities were changed from female into male. According to W.R. Smith,[16] even in historical times the goddesses of the ancient Semites were still in the process of being redefined as gods. The old deities were not easily abandoned, however, for it takes more than religious disapproval to extinguish beliefs and practices which have become entrenched over the passage of time.

Between the fourth and eighth centuries AD Christianity and Islam came to dominate the Middle East. To some extent these male-centred religions which replaced paganism had to bow before the strength of their predecessor. They did this by appropriating certain pagan rites and adapting them to their own beliefs, thereby often reversing their original meaning. Thus Christians have come to celebrate Easter, whose origin was a spring fertility festival in honour of Eastre, the Saxon Queen of Heaven, while Christmas itself is an adaptation of the pagan Saturnalia. The date of Christ's birth was fixed as 25 December to coincide with the festival of the winter solstice, the birth of the sun. This ritual of nativity, once celebrated in Egypt and Syria, derives from the ancient Persian religion of Mithraism, a faith once so powerful throughout the East that it was a serious rival to Christianity.

In order to establish themselves, both Christianity and Islam had to destroy the rituals connected with goddess worship. Thus they attempted to eradicate female dance related to the celebration of sexuality and fertility. (It has even been suggested that the Islamic proscription on naturalistic representation and image-making arose from the repression of female idol worship.) Perhaps for this reason we find little mention of women dancing in the Bible, though frequent reference is made to the men's dance.

A rare Biblical reference to a woman dancing occurs in the New Testament tale of Salome, one of Christianity's adaptations of pagan myth, which has become one of the great themes of dance. Salome's story is based on a myth concerning Ishtar, the Babylonian goddess of love and fertility. In an allegory on the death and rebirth of nature, Ishtar's lover dies and is taken down to the underworld, which also represents the fruitful womb of the earth. Ishtar is so distraught that, dressed in all her finery, she sets out to bring him back. In order to enter the most secret chambers of the underworld she has to pass through seven-times-seven gates, and at each set of gates, as the price of admission, she divests herself of a jewel and a veil. While she is absent from the earth no crops grow, nor is there love or rejoicing of any kind. Only when she returns with her lover does nature blossom forth again after the barren months of winter.

The 'Dance of the Veils of Ishtar', which became known as the 'Welcome Dance' or the 'Dance of Shalome' (from the Hebrew greeting *shalom*), was rewritten in the Bible and its meaning reversed. In the original myth, Ishtar brings back life; in the Bible Salome takes life. Her mother, Herodias, uses Salome to take revenge on John the Baptist for declaring her marriage to Herod invalid. It is Herodias who instructs Salome to dance for Herod on his birthday, and when the king offers Salome anything up to half his kingdom in reward, it is Herodias who prompts Salome to ask for the head of John the Baptist, who has been imprisoned by Herod. The story thus reinforces the Christian emphasis not on a beneficial female magic but on the dark, destructive side of woman's power.

All mass faiths sooner or later tend towards distortion and excess, while original beliefs quickly lose the purity of their message. It is like whispering

a story in someone's ear; once it has gone along the line and been whispered in a dozen ears it has become a different story altogether.

In the mythic pattern there is no creation without sacrifice. In nearly every agrarian religion there is evidence of human sacrifice, which in time became merely symbolic. The rite of human sacrifice culminated in the body being cut into pieces and buried in the fields to fertilize the earth. Any remains were burnt and the ashes strewn over the land. Sacrifice connected with goddess worship came to include the voluntary castration of men and the burying of male organs as a fertility offering. As time passed, these rituals became increasingly excessive. The great spring festival held at the temple of the Syrian goddess Astarte at Hierapolis was presided over by eunuch priests who, urged on by chanting, singing and drumming, would slash their bodies with knives; the religious excitement would give way to a contagious euphoria and men, carried away by the primal power of the music and the mounting frenzy of the crowd, would castrate themselves, using swords which stood ready for the purpose.[17]

Perhaps it was partly the excesses of goddess worship which encouraged men to revolt against the power of women in society. Whatever the case, the dark side of female sexuality has always been an element of ancient legend. In the new male-centred religions of the Middle East, distrust and fear of female sexuality loomed large and were responsible for the move to curtail women's freedom and uproot all customs connected with the faith through which they derived their ancient power. The extent of this fear and distrust, and an indication of how far Christianity had diverged from the ancient view of sex as a sacred duty is shown in St Paul's remarks that by even touching a woman a man defiled himself, and that celibacy was the ideal state for humanity.

The separation of body and spirit is a central axiom of Christianity. Fasting, self-castigation and deprivation of all kinds were practised to subdue the demands of the body and attain a state of pure spirituality, and if all attempts to subjugate the flesh failed, castration was performed. Thus, yet another custom connected with goddess worship was retained by the usurping faith and given a new justification.

Facing page:
The terrible mother; Indian goddess Kali with the heads of her victims around her neck. Modern poster. Bombay

37

Goddess worship gradually disappeared, along with its attendant rituals, and in many places the old fertility dances became only a memory. Where this type of dance remained, it lost its religious significance and became a secular activity, an entertainment and later an artform created for the purposes of observation rather than participation. Over the years, in the hands of professional performers, it developed different forms according to the places where it was still found, such as Africa and Polynesia.

Along the north coast of Africa, in the countries bordering the southern and eastern shores of the Mediterranean, and in the desert lands of the Middle East this dance underwent a fascinating evolution. There, in what has become the Arab-Islamic world, a secular art of great skill and variety was fashioned by women, taking the basic pelvic movement as their starting-point. Although this secular entertainment has no conscious connection with the ancient fertility dance from which it derives, a powerful vestige of its ancestry still clings to it.

In Cairo one night, staying in a hotel whose huge, dusty rooms and ornate pillars betokened a former grandeur, I was attracted by the sound of music coming from the floor below. I slipped downstairs and peered into the ballroom where I found a wedding party in progress, with a cabaret dancer going through her routine. Seeing me with my nose pressed up against the glass, one of the guests opened the door and, with customary Egyptian hospitality, invited me in. The dancer looked tired and bored. She was merely going through her paces, her mind already on the next job. She turned her head and muttered a few words over her shoulder to her musicians. They took up the cue and the dance ended in a grand finale of drumming and spinning. A photographer came and led her away, positioning her between the bride and groom, sitting on the dais in their Western-style wedding outfits. They each placed a hand on her bare belly, everyone smiled and the ritual closed with the flash of the camera.

Chapter 2

THE GYPSY TRAIL

Life is like a ghaziya, *she dances just briefly for each.*

Egyptian proverb

In Egyptian villages a professional dancer is known as a *ghaziya* (pl. *ghawazee*). The original *ghawazee* were gypsies, though the word has come to be used as a generic term for dancers rather than to denote a particular tribe, or tribes, as was once the case. The important role played by gypsies in the development of secular dance is reflected in the Turkish language, whose old word for 'female dancer' (*cengi*) derives from *cingene* (gypsy). The Egyptian *ghawazee* means 'invaders', or 'outsiders', and gypsies have indeed always lived on the outskirts of town and on the fringes of society.

Gypsies of all lands share a common origin in India and a common language in Romany, which is based on Hindi. There are still low-caste Indian tribes who find no place in society and continue to lead a nomadic life in the north-west of the country. The heart of gypsy belief and superstition is the Hindu religion, their patron saint the Indian goddess Kali, the 'Black Madonna' (known by European gypsies as 'Sarah the Egyptian').

The original gypsy tribes left India in the fifth century AD in search of work, and to escape from the many famines and hardships of life. Some were banished, like the Kathaka, travelling minstrels from Sind who went north and became resident court entertainers. There they enjoyed a comfortable lifestyle until they were caught stealing from the imperial treasury and were expelled from the country. Yousef Maazin, father of the most famous present-day *ghawazee*, who live near the temples of Luxor, recounts how his tribe originally came from Persia. He admits that they were cast out of their homeland because of their thieving and generally bad reputation and says they encouraged their daughters and sons to become entertainers in order to settle in Egypt.

The first gypsy tribes migrated west through Afghanistan and Persia, and on the eastern shores

C.R. Huber. *Gypsies of the Sa'id, Egypt.* c.1870. Engraving

Etienne Dinet. *Algerian women accompanying a dance with rhythmic handclapping*. 1900. Watercolour. Private collection

of the Mediterranean their ways divided. Some continued in a northerly direction via Turkey into Europe, while others followed the southern coastline to Egypt. It is believed that they reached Spain via the northern shores of Africa, though only a few isolated gypsy communities have been found along this route. Some think they entered Spain through France, yet Andalusian gypsies believe they came from Egypt. Nomadic tribes of gypsies who neither speak Arabic nor follow Islam can still be found in the oasis of Fayyum in the Nile Delta. Here they continue to lead a life of wandering, travelling with other nomads in order to disguise their identity and avoid persecution.

As outsiders who refuse to conform to the values of society, gypsies have always met hostility in the countries where they have settled. For hundreds of years they have made their living as public performers. They have no written history; instead, their story has been kept alive and transmitted from generation to generation by means of music, song and dance, which hold a special place in their lives. There are two kinds of gypsy entertainment: one remains private, the other has shaped their public repertoire. Music and dance are binding elements in their culture and are used as a means of mocking the pretensions of polite society — whose members they then go on to entertain in their homes.

The Persian poet Firdusi describes how the fifth-century King Bahram brought nearly 1,000 gypsies to Persia to entertain his subjects, who had been complaining that the pleasures of dance and music were reserved for the wealthy. Yet even though he encouraged them to settle, and to this end provided them with cattle, seed corn and asses, they preferred to continue their wandering life. They simply ate the cattle and corn and moved on when the fancy took them.

When they did settle, however, gypsies assimilated the local traditions and made them their own. They took native folk dance and music, amplified and polished them, and then went on to use them as a means of livelihood.

As we have seen, with the suppression of paganism came the suppression of dance. When an activity fulfils basic human needs it is not easily abandoned, however, and beyond the borders of civilization dance traditions continued largely unaltered among the general population. In the classical world dance was separated from the mainstream of life; on the one hand, it was a carefully regulated private activity, and on the other, it was the work of professionals.

Secular dance was developed not only by gypsies, but by other minority groups and the poor. It was partly this association with the lower orders that made it an activity deemed unworthy of 'respectable' citizens. There was another reason, too. By its very nature, dance is an activity which heightens the senses and lowers inhibitions. (The nineteenth-century physician Havelock Ellis, who made a study of human sexual behaviour, commented in a different context, 'A girl who has waltzed for a quarter of an hour is in the same condition as if she had drunk champagne.') Dance was not an activity fit for sober citizens anxious to retain their dignity and self-possession, although it was acceptable if used for the purpose of exercise.

According to the Greek philosopher Aristotle, writing in the third century BC, if music and dance were carefully regulated, they could serve as moral training and give aesthetic gratification of the highest order. However, he cautioned, no citizen should pursue these arts to such an extent that they approached professional status; similarly, no citizen should learn to play a musical instrument. In ancient Greece all professional activity in this field belonged to slaves, freedmen and foreigners.

At the beginning of the first century BC the Roman orator Cicero noted dryly, 'No one dances while he is sober unless he happens to be a lunatic.' It was nevertheless the Romans who instituted dance academies, where it appears that some citizens attained a greater degree of competence than was considered altogether proper. In the fourth century AD the Latin historian Macrobius commented:

> Between the two Punic wars, free-born citizens, even sons of senators, went to dancing schools... I hesitate to say that even married ladies thought dancing no disgrace. On the contrary, even the most respectable took an interest in it, although they did not seek to become experts.[18]

Banwali and Lal. *Indian Kathak entertainers at the marriage of Bagi Muhammad Khan.* Early 16th century. Watercolour. Victoria & Albert Museum, London

Eugène Pavy. *Egyptian musicians.*
c.1850. Oil painting. Private collection

Despite people's reservations, dance remained an indispensable means of animating private festivities. In this context, a conscious consideration of technique and aesthetic values gradually came into being and dance became the art of the individual, who took pleasure in displaying his or her own particular virtuosity and innovations.

The unending upheavals of history, the vanishing and shifting of peoples through successive periods of change, have left their mark on dance the world over. It is not always possible to ascertain which stylistic elements are indigenous to a particular dance and which are the influence of migrant groups, though it is interesting to speculate how dance movements may have travelled from country to country; how a similar use of the body in two otherwise differing dance forms has allowed certain movements to enrich the repertoire of both.

Sinuous arms and a side-to-side sliding of the head on the neck are common movements of Indian, Persian, Turkish and Arabic dance. Finger gestures, each having a particular significance, are an essential characteristic of Indian dance, as well as that of the Algerian Hoggar region and southern Morocco. In Andalusia we find flamenco, whose name is popularly thought to derive from a mispronunciation of the Arabic *fellah* and *mengu*, meaning 'fugitive peasant'. Flamenco is a combination of gypsy and Spanish dance movements with a strong underlying Oriental flavour, which derives partly from the Moorish occupation of Andalusia from the seventh century to the end of the fifteenth. Yet there are certain elements of flamenco which are neither North African, European, nor Middle Eastern in origin, and appear to come directly from India — elements such as the controlled footwork and the way movement rises from the hips to the outstretched arms. The 'Zambra Mora' (Moorish dance) is a little-known form of flamenco that is particularly Oriental in feel. The women's dance of Spanish gypsies, performed at special private gatherings, uses very similar hip movements to those of Arabic dance. It is known as *la danza serpiente* (snake dance), a name which, interestingly enough, is also used by the Spanish to refer to the Arab dance of women.

The use, or playing down, of a particular part of the body in dance is related to taboos as well as aesthetic values. Yet how and why it was North African and Middle Eastern women — as opposed to those of other areas — who retained the old fertility dance and made of it such a sophisticated art remains a mystery.

Arabic dance is characterized by its intricate hip movements which, to judge from fragments of description down the years, have changed little in essence in the last 1,000 years or so, although they have been augmented and refined. Gypsies were not the only ones responsible for the dissemination of this dance, despite the fact that they played a major part in its development. Women who travelled with the invading armies of successive colonial powers also had a hand in taking it from country to country.

The armies of the Roman Empire (27 BC–AD 476) spread out across the Mediterranean into Egypt and Arabia, North Africa and Europe. Whatever their qualms about dance as an activity for respectable citizens, the Romans appreciated it as a diversion, and around 60 BC they imported dancers from Syria to entertain them. Propertius, the greatest elegiac poet of ancient Rome, mentions women being hired to enliven a banquet, where 'they danced lascivious dances to the sound of flutes, and accompanied themselves with castanets'.

The Romans' greatest enthusiasm, however, was reserved for the dancers of Cadiz (Gadez, as it was then known), a town which had been a Phoenician colony before it came under the sway of Rome. Its dancers were celebrated by several Roman writers, including Ovid, who has left the following description: 'Graceful her arms, moving in subtle measure; insinuating she sways her hips'. Juvenal described dancers who 'sink to the ground and quiver with applause… a stimulus for languid lovers, nettles to whip rich men to live', while the poet Martial recorded seeing them 'swing lascivious loins in practised writhings'. This dance was enjoyed from one end of the Roman Empire to the other.

By the end of the first century AD performers had organized into companies in Egypt and other countries of the East. The following extract from a papyrus in the possession of Cornell University includes a contract between an Egyptian performer and her employer:

Turkish cengis entertaining in the harem. c.1850. Postcard of oil painting. Private collection

Facing page:
Persian mutrube. Qajar dynasty, early
19th century. Oil panel. Victoria &
Albert Museum, London

Entertainment in a Persian palace.
1850. Engraving after a painting by
Auguste Shoefft

Syrian peasant girls. 1860. Engraving.
Illustrated London News

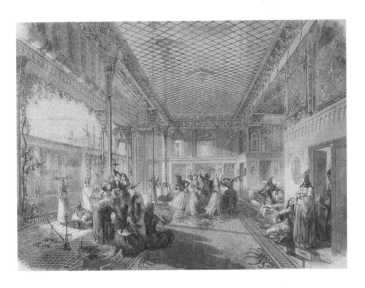

To Isidora, castanet dancer, from Artemisia of the village of Philadelphia. I request that you, assisted by another castanet dancer — total two — undertake to perform at the festival of my house for six days beginning the 24th of the month Payni according to the old calendar, you [two] to receive as pay 36 drachma for each day, and we to furnish in addition 4 artabas of barley and 24 pairs of bread loaves, and on condition further that, if garments or gold ornaments are brought down, we will guard these safely, and that we will furnish you with two donkeys when you come down to us and a like number when you go back to the city.[19]

The payment of dancers reflected the status of their patron as well as the skill of individual performers, and the esteem in which entertainers in general were held by society. At one end of the scale we find Egyptian dancers during the fourth dynasty (2680-2560 BC) being rewarded with gold necklaces and precious jewels. In complete contrast were those dancers who performed in the market-place and whose reward consisted of coins tossed at their feet by passers-by, a tradition which has continued down to the present day. Having nowhere safe to stow their earnings, the dancers incorporated them into their dresses, sewing the coins onto the material itself as part of a bodice or head covering, and onto the shawls which they wore round their hips. Another solution was to convert the money into jewellery which could be worn at all times.

In Arabic dance today, the tinkling of bracelets, anklets, pendants and coin-fringed headscarves provides a festive addition to the musical accompaniment, while the gold and silver sequins covering a modern dance costume have developed directly out of this old tradition of a dancer wearing her wages on her body. Sometimes the performer may lean over in a backbend and invite members of the audience to stick a coin to her forehead, cheeks or lips. In certain areas where Arabic dance is seen, this ritual still remains part of the performance, with some of a dancer's earnings coming to her directly from her audience in the form of tips, solicited or otherwise.

Further up the scale of professional dancers were

those hired by individuals for private celebrations. At the top of the hierarchy in Persia, India, Egypt and Turkey were troupes of entertainers who were retained as part of the royal household. Immense rewards were often lavished on a sovereign's favourite dancers:

> So unbounded are the payments thus made to these performers that some of the ancient and most powerful Persian and Mogul dynasties are said to have owed their decline and fall to such extravagances.[20]

Entertainment is a favourite subject of miniatures from the nineteenth-century Persian Qajar dynasty. The ceramic tiles decorating the 'hose' (a small fountain for the ritual washing before prayer) often

Court celebration. 19th century. Persian ceramic tile. Tehran Ethnological Museum

depicted scenes of revelry, complete with dishes of fruit, flagons of wine and a company of dancers parading across them. In the second half of the nineteenth century, while on a trip to Europe, Shah Nasir ed-Dini became so fascinated by the costume of ballerinas that he insisted it be adopted by his own dancers, as well as by the ladies of the royal household. As can be seen from Persian figurative painting prior to the 1860s, dancers had previously worn floor-length flared dresses with wide pantaloons underneath and a slender girdle at the waist, hanging down in front. Their new ballet-inspired outfits, with knee-length skirts and a virtually transparent chemise, were regarded as a shocking innovation. One nobleman commented, 'There are two classes of Persian women who wear that unseemly European attire: those who can afford to lose their decency, and those who do not even know they have any decency to lose.'[21]

Dancers did not always live at court. Some of them were brought in for special occasions. Others, generally slaves, were members of the royal harem and were the concubines of rulers and their male relatives. They were highly trained in the arts and, as was generally the case with the most elevated courtesan-dancers, were often the only educated women in their society. (This was also true of the ancient Greek *hetairae*, the Japanese geisha and the dancers of classical India.) They boasted the skills of reading and writing, as well as being good conversationalists and accomplished singers, musicians and dancers. These women were well regarded and some of them owned property bestowed on them by their patrons.

Shaikh Abd al-Rahman al-Djabarti tells of an Egyptian singer who lived in Cairo at the beginning of the Fatimid dynasty. When the Fatimid al-Moezz entered the conquered city in AD 969, she and her troupe of musicians greeted him with a song:

> Abbasids, give up your power,
> Moezz has become king.
> The sceptre you held was only a loan,
> And all loans must be repaid.

The new ruler was so pleased that he rewarded her with property in the heart of the city.

Persian costume, pre-1860s. Miniature. The Israel Museum, Jerusalem

Dalvimart. *Turkish cengi with brass finger cymbals.* 1802. Colour engraving. Victoria & Albert Museum, London

Singers, poets and musicians enjoyed the highest status among all female entertainers, partly due to the fact that, unlike dancers, they veiled themselves and observed a modest demeanour in public. In Egypt they became known as *awalim* (sing. *almeh*), or 'learned women'. When Europeans went to Egypt in the nineteenth century and wrote about entertainers, they often mistakenly referred to a dancer as an *almeh*, but the true *awalim* do not appear to have danced very often, although it seems that dancers sometimes added singing to their repertoire in order to win greater respect. The true *awalim* were highly educated and gifted in all the arts. At weddings their role, along with that of dancers, was to instruct the bride in the art of lovemaking, through the language of song and dance.

One of the nineteenth century's best-known *awalim* was Sakina al-Maz. If she sang for a male audience she would conceal herself behind a screen, recounting her life story in songs which became increasingly impassioned as she was urged on to greater heights by her audience's expressions of enthusiasm and applause. We have a description of Sakina by Lucie Duff Gordon, an Englishwoman who, for health reasons, made her home in Egypt in the 1860s:

> Sakina… is 55 — an ugly face, I am told (she was veiled and one only saw the eyes and glimpses of her mouth when she drank water), but the figure of a leopard, all grace and beauty, and a splendid voice of its kind, harsh but thrilling. I guessed her about 30 or perhaps 35. When she improvised, the finesse and grace of her whole 'Wesen' were ravishing. Sakina was treated with great consideration and quite as a friend by the Armenian ladies with whom she talked between her songs. She is a Muslimeh and very rich and charitable. She gets £50 for a night's singing at least.[22]

According to another outside observer of the same period, the German writer Georg Moritz Ebers, the *awalim* began their careers in the houses of the wealthy, and when their voices lost their freshness and charm they retired into private life. It was not uncommon for them to take the name of their patron and remain connected with him for life. Otherwise they married and continued their careers, with their husbands acting as their managers and general organizers. The less-elevated *awalim* sang, and also danced, in public. As an indication of their prestige, when the dancers were banished from Cairo in 1834 (see ch.3), the singers were allowed to remain.

Huda Shaarawi, a leader of the Egyptian feminist movement, recalls a travelling poetess who visited her house when she was a child in Cairo in the 1890s:

> Sayyida Khadija impressed me because she used to sit with the men and discuss literary and cultural matters. Meanwhile I observed how women without learning would tremble with embarrassment and fright if called upon to speak a few words to a man from behind a screen.[23]

In general, the status of entertainers depended on the social position of their patrons and was always precarious. For even if they enjoyed prestige and favour early on in their careers, there was no guarantee that they would not fall from grace or be discarded when their skill and beauty began to fade. One method of insurance against the vagaries of fortune was to band together in a company. The *cengis* of Turkey were well organized in this respect, with an older member of the troupe acting as business manager for the entire company. In this way they managed a degree of protection enjoyed by few independent female entertainers.

The public's attitude towards professional dancers in North Africa and the Middle East has always been ambiguous. A principal reason is that dance is frowned on by Islam, the dominant faith in the Arab world. Muhammad's original aim was to convert only the people of his native city, Mecca, from paganism. However, as a crusading faith, Islam overspilled its original boundaries and in Muhammad's own lifetime was taken into Arabia. After his death in AD 632, successive waves of conquest took the faith to other parts of the world. In the seventh century Syria, Egypt and Tunisia were brought under Arab control, followed by Algeria and Morocco. At the beginning of the eighth century the Moors conquered southern Spain, where they established a civilization of great

Lorie. *Egyptian almeh, Sakina al-Maz.* c.1870. Engraving

Gagarin. *Turkish bayadere.* c.1850.
Watercolour. Victoria & Albert
Museum, London

wealth and learning which has left an indelible
impression on the arts of Spain. By the ninth century
Persia and nearly the whole of India were dominated
by the Muslims.

In Islamic thought the sacred and the secular are
indissolubly linked. It follows that recreational
pursuits have to be reconciled with ethical principles.
Since this was not possible with all types of dance,
the safest solution was to condemn the art in its
entirety. There was, however, another reason for
condemning female dancing in public. A basic tenet
of Islam is that women should not display their bodies
in the presence of strangers. Dancers were the only
women who transgressed this law and appeared
unveiled in public, which in the Islamic world is the
men's domain.

Professional performers belonged to communities
who often paid lip service to Islamic custom, while
maintaining their old beliefs. As far as female dance
is concerned, there have always been fewer taboos
governing women's appearance in public among
gypsies and those removed from the constraints of
urban dwelling, such as the desert bedouin.

Flouting convention, the dancers became the
principal public expression of sensual joy and beauty,
and so they have remained. In many countries of
the ancient East, dancers were thought to bring
good fortune, for something of the old 'divine' power
of temple dancers clung to them. They were
considered to have an essential role in all public and
private celebrations, for besides bringing good
fortune, they animated the festivities. Performing
for a wealthy patron, they took on something of a
surrogate role, indulging in an activity their audience
was denied and could only enjoy vicariously as
spectators.

In a sense, Islamic condemnation of public dancing
by 'respectable' women was advantageous for the
new professional entertainers, opening up a place
for them in society which could not have been filled
by anyone else. Some managed to cross the dividing-
line into the respectable world themselves. In pre-
Islamic times the most famous woman to do so was
a dancer-courtesan of humble origins named
Theodora. In AD 527 she married the Emperor
Justinian and became the power behind the throne
in the Byzantine Empire.

Today those dancers who are recognized for their artistry earn considerable sums of money and are accepted into the ranks of their wealthy patrons, while the vast number of less skilled dancers continue to bear the stigma of their profession. There are, however, common benefits enjoyed by all dancers in the Arab-Islamic world which counteract their precarious position on the fringes of society. Their status as breadwinners inevitably lends them a certain self-confidence and authority. Moreover, their profession allows them a freedom of behaviour not permitted other women, a fact which is reflected in popular descriptions of them. The Moroccan *chikhat*, who perform in troupes and travel from place to place entertaining at family festivities, are known as 'women who do not want men to tell them what to do'. As dancers, they are not necessarily denied marriage and the rewards of a family, and indeed, their male relatives may be dependent on them for their livelihood. It is an interesting reversal of the normal order, in which, by being confined to the home with a man as breadwinner, Muslim women are considered in their own society to be protected from the harsh realities of a cruel world. We may draw a parallel with the Indian courtesan-dancers who live in Bombay, in the compound of Pavanpul. There, contrary to normal custom, the birth of a girl is celebrated and she is trained from infancy in her future profession. The men of the community spend their days in idleness, sitting in cafés smoking and playing cards; only those with musical skills are valued as possible wage-earners.

In an interview some time before his death, Yousef Maazin said that he was lucky to have been blessed with so many beautiful daughters, for they had provided him with a handsome living. (In the Arab world a family generally hopes for the birth of a son rather than a daughter.) Maazin allowed his unmarried daughters the pleasure of male companionship in the home as a ploy to discourage them from marriage, reasoning that if they enjoyed a certain degree of freedom, they would not be over-impatient to marry. For marriage brings a *ghaziya*'s career to an end.

Today the Maazin sisters are famous. In recent years they have been the subject of a number of

Western interviews and documentaries on dance and gypsy life. Yet despite their fame, they are acutely aware that among their own people they are not considered acceptable marriage partners. As one of them has commented:

> The only time I wish I wasn't a dancer is when a man from another tribe falls in love with me or one of my sisters. His family would fight a war to stop him marrying a *ghaziya*. 'How can you marry a daughter of Maazin? A dancer and singer who performs in front of others?' They call us by the name *ghaziya*. To them it's an insult. But to us it means we invade their hearts with our dancing.

Considering the options open to them, dancers in the Arab world are in some respects fortunate. They are not obliged to conform to all the rules of society. Their work gives them social mobility and independence, and though their position may be ambivalent, that in itself can be a kind of freedom.

Chapter 3

A CHARM BEYOND BEAUTY

*It was profoundly dramatic, a lyric of love which words
cannot tell.*

G.W. Curtis

Europe and the Arab world have a relationship which long predates Christianity and Islam. Under the Roman Empire they were part of the same political system, while the flow of ideas between them has existed for thousands of years. As a result the West has absorbed many elements of Eastern thought, principal among them being the concept of sacred monarchy, derived from the Persian religion of Mithraism, in which the king is equated with the sun. A further indication of the debt which Western civilization owes to the East is that for nearly 2,000 years, after its own pagan faith was usurped, the West has, in Christianity, followed a religion which originated in the Middle East.

Like Christianity, Islam is a crusading faith, and having registered considerable conquests in other parts of the world, came close to conquering Europe when Berber and Arab forces reached southern Spain in the ninth century. The threat of Islamic colonialism was one factor which sparked off the Crusades. Yet at the same time as the Church was preparing to wage war on the East, the European intelligentsia were unstinting in their praise of Arab culture.

Between the tenth and twelfth centuries the Moorish civilization of Andalusia was one of great wealth and elegance. Scholars from all over Europe were drawn to the centres of learning in Cordoba and Seville, meeting-places of civilization where they rediscovered the lost Greek classics in Arabic translation as well as becoming acquainted with the learning of the Islamic world. Mediaeval Christian scholars' enthusiasm for the learning of Islam was largely responsible for a renaissance of European culture in the twelfth century and for the foundation of the first European universities.

Throughout the following centuries European

Ghaziya. c.1839. Tinted
daguerrotype. Private collection

culture continued to draw on Oriental learning where necessary, although never to the same extent as before. Only with the opening of comprehensive trade routes to the East in the seventeenth and eighteenth centuries did a fascination with the cultures of Asia and North Africa return.

In the sixteenth century, a crucial period in the development of European decorative art, a style evolved which owed a great debt to Islamic design. Ornamental art in Europe was naturalistic in character, its effect three-dimensional, basically static and weighty. The two-dimensional arabesque of Islamic art, with its flowing, interlacing lines, gave rhythm and movement to the European tradition and was gradually worked into the classical and Gothic styles to a point where it could no longer be distinguished as an outside influence. The arabesque was suited to crafts of all kinds, metalwork, ceramics, embroidery and textiles, as well as to architecture. Printing, too, benefited from the influence of Islamic design, with the process of marbling (the application of oil colours on water) learned from Turkish artists.

Despite hostilities between Europe and the Middle East in the late mediaeval and early Renaissance periods, trade between them continued and craftsmen were able to collect and study the fine arts of the East. In Holbein's portraits of Tudor kings and queens, Oriental rugs can be seen draped over the furniture, hanging from the walls, even luxuriously laid on the floor. These carpets became increasingly popular among the more affluent members of society, and from 1600 onwards were produced in Persia and Turkey especially for European markets. From the late seventeenth century various household artefacts, modes of dress and social customs from the East became a feature of life in European society, from coffee houses and Turkish baths to the wearing of turbans.

By the nineteenth century 'Orientalism' was a well-established phenomenon. The Orient was an ill-defined area which included parts of Asia, the Middle East, North Africa and the Mediterranean. It was a part of the world with which the West had previously had only intermittent contact, mainly through traders, political adventurers and wealthy travellers.

The nineteenth-century focus of interest was the Middle East, much of it ruled by the Turkish Ottomans, whose empire at its height stretched from Vienna to the Yemen and embraced parts of Africa and Asia, lands linked together by the faith of Islam. However, as the Ottomans' hold over their possessions began to weaken, and as European power grew, communities in different parts of the Middle East began to look to Europe for protection and alliances.

The current, widely held view of Orientalism derives from Edward Said's thesis that the West has exploited, misunderstood and even invented the East for its own sinister purposes.[24] From the wealth of material available, it is easy to select examples to suit this theory and ignore those which do not. However, Orientalist attitudes to the Middle East are as varied as human beings. An obsession with European colonialism has unfortunately blinded many critics to the complex interrelationship which has existed between Europe and the Arab-Islamic world for hundreds of years. This obsession has merely served to prolong the misunderstanding which exists between them. Many Europeans who went to the Arab world compared the life they found there favourably with that of Europe. On a visit to North Africa in 1832, the French painter Delacroix wrote of the Moroccans:

> They are closer to nature in a thousand ways — their dress, the form of their shoes. And so beauty has a share in everything they make. As for us in our corsets, our tight shoes, our ridiculous pinching clothes, we are pitiful.[25]

In August 1762 the German explorer Carsten Niebuhr took part in a Danish expedition to the Yemen. While waiting in Cairo for a boat to take them on the next stage of their journey, he and his crew paid some dancers to entertain them. As the crew were all unmarried, the dancers were forbidden to perform for them in private, so the entertainment took place in front of their hotel:

> At first we did not greatly appreciate this kind of entertainment, for the music was quite poor and the women immodest, to our way of

thinking. They exposed themselves in front of us in every way, and we found them ugly, with their dyed yellow hands and blood-red fingernails. The black and blue necklaces and big heavy anklets, the rings in their ears and noses, and the rich use of grease in their hair was not to our taste at all. However, little by little we changed our minds and found them beautiful, even to the extent that we enjoyed their entertainment as much as we would have enjoyed seeing the finest dancers and singers in Europe.[26]

This account is one of the earliest Western descriptions we have of the dancers, who were to become one of the greatest sources of fascination for subsequent travellers. Some thirty years after Niebuhr's encounter with the dancers, the first organized European expedition to Egypt took place, when in 1798 Napoleon set out on his ill-fated voyage to Egypt. This date, which marked the beginning of an accelerating Western interest in the Arab world, can conveniently be taken as indicating the start of the Orientalist era.

Ghawazee entertaining travellers by torchlight in Asiut. Mid-19th century. Engraving. *Arabesque* collection, New York

Engelmann. *A dance at Benisouef.*
c.1850. Lithograph

When Napoleon set sail for Egypt he took with him a team of scholars to study the country's culture and achievements from ancient to modern times. His occupation of Egypt proved short-lived, but the massive *Description de l'Egypte* produced by his team has proved of enduring worth and was responsible for stimulating enormous interest in the Middle East.

In Cairo Napoleon's soldiers encountered the *ghawazee*, who lived in al-Hhoshe Derbek (Street of the Open Hall), along with other non-gypsy tribes who earned their living as entertainers. In the daily social intercourse between these people, it is possible that women from different tribes picked up each other's skills, and in this way developed a dance which owed something to both Egyptian and gypsy dance.

Those *ghawazee* who did not live in Cairo camped along the banks of the Nile. They travelled about a good deal, and at the spring and autumn festivals the Delta would be dotted with their multi-coloured tents. We are told that they were one of the principal

Previous page:
Leopold Carl Müller. *Ghaziya from the Sa'id, Egypt.* Mid-19th century. Oil painting. Mathaf Gallery, London

Facing page, top:
Luigi Mayer. *Dancers with tribal tattoos.* 1801. Aquatint. Victoria & Albert Museum, London

Facing page, bottom:
David Roberts. *Ghawazee, Cairo.* 1842. Colour lithograph. Victoria & Albert Museum, London

attractions of these festivals, and that monkey trainers who taught their animals a parody of *ghawazee* dancing exhibited them with great success at the *mouleds* (popular religious feasts in honour of saints).

As we have seen, the reputation of professional dancers varied according to the social status of their audience. Those who performed for the wealthy and the ruling elite were highly regarded, as well as being wealthy themselves. Some of them owned property, animals and even slaves, professed faith in Islam and accompanied the pilgrimage to Mecca. At the opposite end of the scale were those who earned their living from a combination of dancing and prostitution. They lived apart from society and married within their own tribe. Marriage did not put an end to their dancing, however; indeed, their husbands were financially dependent on them and often acted for them in the capacity of musician and manager.

The *ghawazee*, like many who live by their wits on the fringes of society, knew several languages and had a secret code of their own, which was not understood by outsiders. The dancers could be found performing in public squares, in cafés and on the steps of hotels. Unlike the *awalim*, they were not invited to 'respectable' harems. The *awalim* left Cairo during Napoleon's occupation of the city, refusing to entertain his soldiers. The *ghawazee*, on the other hand, fraternized with the French. Napoleon's generals, blaming them for creating unrest, recommended that they should be severely punished if they did not keep away from the barracks. According to the French writer Auriant, the women were not deterred by this threat. As a result, 400 of them were seized and decapitated and their headless bodies thrown into the Nile.

Less barbaric, though more definitive in doing away with their presence, in 1834 the *ghawazee* were outlawed from Cairo. Muhammad Ali, an Albanian adventurer, had seized power in Egypt in 1799 and had embarked on the modernization of the country with the help of European advisers. Religious pressure, added to the notoriety of the dancers, led him to banish them to Upper Egypt where they settled in the towns of Esna, Aswan and Kean. Any woman who defied the ban was liable to fifty lashes for a first offence and hard labour for any further infringement of the law.

It appears that some dancers disobeyed the edict, though they carried on their profession with a good deal of secrecy and stealth. Many a traveller noted that it was always possible to find them if one looked hard enough, and the American traveller Charles Leland,[27] writing in the 1870s, commented that, despite the ban, it remained fashionable among the wealthy to enliven their parties with dancers. He added that most travellers, if given the choice, would rather have seen the dancing than the pyramids.

The French author Charles Didier was of this opinion, though he found it difficult to satisfy his curiosity:

> I was consumed with a desire to see them. God knows how much I had searched, how many inquiries I had made into the matter. I had asked the help of others, some of them very important, powerful people, but all I had received were a lot of beautiful promises, not one of which had been fulfilled. Hari-Bey himself not only promised to close his eyes to the illegality, but to help and advise me, but even his tolerance, that is, his protection and influence, were not enough to get any results.
>
> The few dancers remaining in Cairo were so frightened that they did not dare to come out of hiding; not one was willing, at any price, to expose herself to the dangers of arrest. As long as they were under my roof, or in the home of any other European, they were safe, but the police, alerted by the sound of the *tars* and the dancers' finger cymbals, might be waiting outside for them.[28]

Eventually, quite by accident, Didier met an *almeh* who took him to her home, where she sang and danced for him. When he confessed his desire to see the *ghawazee* dance she agreed, albeit reluctantly, to arrange an entertainment for him. Delighted, he went off to make the necessary arrangements, which consisted of hiring a boat and buying provisions for the night's festivities. On the day of the party he went to meet the *almeh* as arranged. But she did not appear, and though he

Sword dance at Jericho. c.1870. Lithograph

Previous page:
Jean-Léon Gérôme. *An almeh performing the sword dance.* c.1870. Oil painting. Herbert & Johnson Museum, Cornell University, New York

Luigi Mayer. *Celebration at Ned Sili.* 1801. Aquatint. Private collection

spent most of the day and night waiting for her he never saw her again. Some time later he learned that, following their first meeting, the *almeh* had been arrested and imprisoned. After being whipped 'for having had relations with a Christian', she was taken up the Nile to join the other dancers.

The English painter James Augustus St John was more fortunate than Didier. In 1845 in a little village near Cairo, a group of young girls aged from 10 to 16 entertained him in a coffee house. The girls generally spent most of their time there, drinking, singing and engaging in:

> that sort of piquant conversation which becomes their calling... Coffee appeared to produce in them the same excitement and petulant gaiety to which champagne and burgundy sometimes give birth among European women.

In Cairo he witnessed another performance, this time at the home of a wealthy Armenian living within sight of the pyramids:

> Suddenly the musicians, who had hitherto gratified us only with fantasias of various kinds, and Arab melodies, struck up a dancing measure: the door was opened, and two Arab

dancers entered. They were girls between the ages of 16 and 30, tall and admirably proportioned.

There was something ladylike in their not very dark faces; especially their sharply cut eyebrows, arching finely over their sparkling eyes, and their delicately formed mouths were full of grace and witchery.

Their eyes shot fire; their bosoms heaved and panted, and their bodies assumed the most varied attitudes and inflexions. They twined round each other snake-like, with a suppleness and grace such as I had never seen before. Now, they let their arms drop, and their whole frames seemed to collapse in utter exhaustion; then might you see how a new thought arose within them, and strove to express itself in impassioned gestures. All this while the music continued to play, and in its very simplicity was like a pale background to the picture, from which the glowing figures of the girls stood out in so much the stronger relief.

After a pause, the second dance began. One of the *ghawazee* took a little glass, filled it with rose water, between her teeth, and held it so without spilling a drop, whilst she executed the most rapid and difficult movements. She repeated nearly the whole of the preceding dance, and it was certainly no trifling effort of skill to go through it without emptying the glass. At last, she stepped up to one of the male spectators, and clasping him round the middle with both arms, she bent backwards, and continued her gesticulations without ceasing; at last she leaned forward, and slowly poured the rose water over his clothes, let the glass drop, kissed his lips, and bounded back into the middle of the room.[29]

Many descriptions of Arabic dance from the 1860s and 1870s indicate that the women's solo dance, *baladi*, was the most popular of all. Sometimes it involved mime, sometimes feats of acrobatic skill, such as balancing cups of liquid on the head, and even swords, as can be seen in a painting by Jean-Léon Gérôme. Writers commented on the basic isolation and control of different parts of the body,

Prisse d'Avennes. *Ghawazee.* 1848.
Colour lithograph. Victoria & Albert
Museum, London

the upper torso generally remaining motionless, with the face impassive and grave, while the hips described patterns of vigorous, ever-accelerating movement. One writer, comparing the characteristics of Arabic and Western dance, noted, 'The upper body of the *almeh* dances a solemn minuet, while the rest of her person is worthy to figure in a wild quadrille.'[30]

Leland observed of the *ghawazee*:

> They all seem to have the power of moving any part of the body freely, just as certain persons can move their ears; and it is wonderful how they will continue to agitate every muscle in the most violent and rapid manner for hours, quivering from head to foot as if electrified, without being in the least fatigued and, what is incredible, without perspiring.[31]

The splendour of their dresses provoked frequent comment. The English historian E.W. Lane tells us that they wore in public the same costume that middle-class Egyptian women wore in the privacy of the harem.[32] D'Avennes' portrait of two *ghawazee* performing in a Cairo street shows the basic theme of their dress. As can be seen, they generally wore an undergarment of transparent white muslin with long sleeves which, as they lifted their arms above their heads in the dance, fell back to the elbow, revealing a quantity of gold and silver bracelets. Over this chemise they wore either a long jacket or a bolero-style satin waistcoat, tightly fitting to reveal the contours of their body, with loose, Turkish-style pantaloons gathered in at the ankle and worn low on the hips.

In the portrait, the *ghaziya* on the right wears pantaloons of a patterned material which was probably imported English cotton. Tiger-like stripes were also popular. One or more shawls tied round the hips had the effect of emphasizing the pelvic movement of the dance. As an alternative to these shawls, a dancer might have a strip of bright satin (red was a popular colour) wound tightly round the hips, or a girdle with silver amulets hanging from it.

The overall effect was of layers of colour with masses of silver and gold jewellery as the finishing touch. Leland saw *ghawazee* wearing:

garments of black from head to foot, with silver stripes, while the braids of their hair were very prettily made, terminating in many silver balls. At Assiut I saw one whose only ornaments were an incredible quantity of gold coins of all sizes.[33]

Other *ghawazee* wore only a single strand of pearls in their hair. The Frenchman Charles Blanc, writing in the 1870s, noted a general love of coral and amber:

> Just as the women of Europe like to announce their presence by the rustling of their silk skirts, in the same way the Egyptian women seem to love to listen to the jingling of the ornaments they wear in their ears, on their arms, around their necks, and even on their legs, just above the ankle. This fashion must have been around a long time, because in the Quran there is a passage condemning this type of ostentation: 'Women shall refrain from making noise with their feet when walking, lest they call attention to their ornaments, which should be concealed.'[34]

The *ghawazee* wore a small velvet cap on the crown of the head and braided their hair in ingenious ways, weaving in strings of black silk with gold spangles sewn onto them. The Reverend E. Neil described just how complex their hair dressing could be. At the end of each string of spangles was a multi-faceted gold bead, with gold coins suspended on a ring beneath it. Wealthy women in their homes had anything up to 900 gold ornaments woven into their hair, with tassels of pearls and emeralds at the end of each string of gold spangles. Neil concluded, rather censoriously:

> The countless gold spangles almost entirely hide the hair and glitter and tinkle with every movement of the head. It would be difficult to find in the way of jewellery a vainer or more artificial form of female adornment.[35]

The women used kohl round their eyes, drawing a thin line inside the lower eyelid, and tinted their hands and feet with henna.

In Gérôme's 'Dance of the Almeh' the dancer's breasts are visible beneath her muslin chemise.

James Augustus St John noted that red 'nipple caps' were sometimes worn for private performances in front of foreign men, when the dancers were known to wear only their chemise and pantaloons, together with their jewellery. For such an audience they were sometimes required to appear nude, although they did not like to do so, and agreed to the request with considerable contempt. In such a case, their musicians were blindfolded and Arab men were dismissed from the room.

Lucie Duff Gordon recorded a conversation with the English consul in Cairo, who invited her to dine with him at his home:

> Seyyid Achmet would have given me a fantasia, but he feared that I might have men with me, and he had had a great annoyance with two Englishmen who wanted to make the girls dance naked, which they objected to, and he had to turn them out of his house after hospitably entertaining them.[36]

It is worth noting that it was not only men who demanded that a dancer perform nude for them. Scantily clad dancers were not the norm, however (certainly among those dancers who performed in public places). Even Lane, who referred to the *ghawazee* as 'female warriors against modesty', compared them to the finest women in Egypt, as far as their rich dress was concerned.

In the early 1830s Lane published his exhaustive study on Egyptian life, *An Account of the Manners and Customs of the Modern Egyptians*. This book, the fruit of considerable research, covered every aspect of the subject and came to be considered the definitive text on Muslim life. From Lane we learn that the *ghawazee* contributed over a tenth of all taxes collected in Cairo when they were still in residence and that, as a result of their banishment to Upper Egypt, the citizens of Cairo were subjected to an increase in taxation.

Another result of their banishment was a rise in the number of boy dancers. Many of these *khawals* originally came from Constantinople (Istanbul), where they had been outlawed for causing trouble in the coffee houses. Members of their audiences were known to throw glasses, brandish swords and

Turkish boys imitating the women's dance. 18th century. Miniature. Topkapi Palace Museum, Istanbul

even get into fights over the relative merits of the *khawals*. With the *ghawazee* gone from Cairo, boy dancers grew in number and popularity. They appeared disguised as women, aping the women's dance and, according to some witnesses, made it more salacious than the *ghawazee* had done. Occasionally they were even taken for women by Europeans:

> The dancing girls appeared in a cloud of dust and tobacco smoke. The first thing about them that struck me was the brightness of the golden caps upon their tresses. As their heels beat upon the ground, with a tinkle of little bells and anklets, their raised arms quivered in harmony; their hips shook with a voluptuous movement; their form seemed bare under the muslin between the little jacket and the low, loose girdle, like the belt of Venus. They twirled about so quickly that it was hard to distinguish the features of these seductive creatures, whose fingers shook little cymbals, as large as castanets, as they gestured boldly to the primitive strains of the flute and tambourine. Two of them seemed particularly beautiful; they held themselves proudly: their Arab eyes brightened by kohl, their full yet delicate cheeks were lightly painted. But the third, I must admit, betrayed the less gentle sex by a week-old beard; and when I looked into the matter carefully, and the dance being ended, could better make out the features of the other two, it did not take me long to discover that the dancing girls were, in point of fact, all males.[37]

In 1866 the ban on the *ghawazee* was lifted, and they were allowed to return to Cairo.

A recent work on the Orientalist view of Middle Eastern women quotes exclusively condemnatory comments from the nineteenth century about Arabic dance. The author cites women writers who found it 'disgusting', 'horrid' and 'obscene', but does not mention any of the accounts, by women as well as men, which praised the dance. Lucie Duff Gordon's is one of them. At first she found the dance dull and uninteresting, nothing more than feats of gymnastic skill. But then:

The captain called out to one Latifeh, an ugly, clumsy-looking wench, to show what she could do. And then it was revealed to me. The ugly girl started on her feet and became 'the serpent of the Nile' — the head, shoulders and arms eagerly bent forward, waist in, and haunches advanced on the bent knees, the position of a cobra about to spring. I could not call it voluptuous any more than Racine's *Phaedre*. It is Venus *toute entière à sa proie attachée*, and to me seemed tragic. It is far more realistic than the fandango, and far less coquettish, because the thing represented is *au grand sérieux*, not travestied, *gazé*, or played with; and like all such things, the Arab men don't think it the least improper.[38]

In contrast, she tells us that when two of her Egyptian boatmen were in Paris they were 'dreadfully shocked' by the dancing of the French women.

On a similar note, Leland, who described the dance as 'a charm beyond beauty', compared the *ghaziya* with the European ballerina:

Sometimes two girls dance a duo; and I have seen this made quite as improper, though not as sickly sentimental, as in any opera house in Europe, when the ballerina falls back into the male object's arms, eyeing him with a leering smile, while she lifts one leg to the gallery.[39]

Many of the world's great dances have an erotic element. Yet while this eroticism is only one aspect of Arabic dance, it has unfortunately tended to dominate any discussion on the subject. Nineteenth-century English travellers came from a country in which the pendulum had swung from the riotous bawdy of Georgian times to the covert sexual obsession which characterized Queen Victoria's reign. Preoccupied by that which was forbidden (though none the less readily available) in their own country, many observers saw in Arabic dance only its thrilling eroticism.

Most of the accounts from this period describe anonymous dancers. One of the very few *ghawazee* whom we know by name, and the most famous of her day, was Safiya, who called herself Kutchuk Hanem (Turkish for 'Little Princess'). Kutchuk Hanem was one of a handful of dancers who managed to escape banishment from Cairo, thanks to having a powerful protector. She was at one time the favourite of Muhammad Ali's grandson, Abbas Pasha, who did not bother to hide his association with her:

> One day, as he [Abbas Pasha] was sitting openly with his mistress, smoking in front of her house, a young man, jealous of him, passed by and, certainly not by accident, upset the water pipe of his illustrious rival. This incident was a big scandal in Cairo, where it is still talked about today.[40]

Kutchuk Hanem was foolish enough to let herself be caught selling jewellery — a gift from Abbas Pasha — to a secondhand dealer in the bazaar. On discovering this, her protector gave her a personal flogging and sent her up the Nile to Esna. There in the 1850s the American journalist G.W. Curtis found her. He described her as 'a bud no longer, yet a flower not too fully blown' — in fact she was in her early twenties then — with 'red pulpy lips... lazy, careless, self-possessed'. Curtis's account of his visit to Kutchuk Hanem is the most detailed description which we have of her dancing:

> The sharp surges of sound swept around the room, dashing in regular measure against her movelessness, until suddenly the whole surface of her frame quivered in measure with the music. Her hands were raised, clapping the castanets, and she slowly turned upon herself, her right leg the pivot, marvellously convulsing all the muscles of her body. When she had completed the circuit of the spot on which she stood, she advanced slowly, all the muscles jerking in time to the music, and in solid, substantial spasms.
>
> It was a curious and wonderful gymnastic. There was no graceful dancing — only the movement of dancing when she advanced, throwing one leg before the other as gypsies dance. But the rest was most voluptuous

motion — not the lithe wooing of languid passion, but the soul of passion starting through every sense, and quivering in every limb. It was the very intensity of motion, concentrated and constant... Suddenly stooping, still muscularly moving, Kutchuk fell upon her knees and writhed, with body, arms and head upon the floor, still in measure — still clanking the castanets, and arose in the same manner... Still she retreated, until the constantly down-slipping shawl seemed only just clinging to her hips and making the same circuit upon herself, she sat down, and after this violent and extravagant exertion was marbly cold.[41]

Was Kutchuk Hanem the best of the dancers or simply the best known? Other *ghawazee* were quick to criticize her. Maxime du Camp, who accompanied the French novelist Gustave Flaubert to Egypt in the late 1840s, met one of Kutchuk Hanem's critics, a Nubian dancer called Aziza. While he was sitting in the bazaar in Aswan one day lunching on fresh figs and dates, Aziza came and introduced herself:

> She kissed my hand respectfully and said, 'I am a dancer; my body is suppler than a snake's; if you wish, I can come with my musicians and dance barefoot on the deck of your boat.'
> 'The *cawadja* has seen Kutchuk Hanem at Esna,' Joseph [du Camp's servant] answered her.
> 'Kutchuk Hanem doesn't know how to dance,' she replied.
> I told Joseph to accept; and towards evening, when the setting sun had tempered the heat and shadows spread over the riverbank, the dancer came with her players of the *rebec* and *darabukeh*... Her dance is savage and makes one think involuntarily of the negroes of central Africa. Sometimes she uttered a shrill cry, as though to spur the zeal of her musicians. Between her fingers her noisy castanets tinkled and rang unceasingly... She held out her two long arms, black and glistening, shaking them from shoulder to wrist with an imperceptible quivering, moving them apart with soft and quick motions like those of the wings of a

Facing page:
Edouard Richter. *The soloist.* 19th century. Oil painting. Mathaf Gallery, London

hovering eagle. Sometimes she bent over completely backwards, supporting herself on her hands in the position of the dancing Salome over the left portal of the Rouen cathedral.

'*Cawadja*, what do you think of Kutchuk Hanem now?' she cried.[42]

Flaubert found the way Aziza slid her head from side to side on her neck terrifying, making her look as if she were about to be decapitated. He agreed that her dancing was the most expert that he had seen, yet even so, it was Kutchuk Hanem who made the most lasting impression on him. Flaubert went to visit her twice during his travels. His meticulous travel notes mention every detail of her appearance, from the blue tassels on her *tarboosh*, spreading like a fan over her shoulders, to one of her teeth that was beginning to go bad. He watched her sleep, involuntarily contracting her hands and thighs, and counted the bedbugs on the wall. These bedbugs 'were the most enchanting touch of all. Their nauseating odour mingled with the scent of her skin, which was dripping with sandalwood oil.'

Kutchuk sent away the boatman, covered the eyes of her musicians and danced 'The Bee' for Flaubert. According to his servant Joseph, 'The Bee' was a lost dance, a myth whose name alone survived. He claimed to have seen it once, performed by a man — a superior version, he said, to that of Kutchuk Hanem. With shrill cries to indicate that a bee had somehow found its way into her clothes and' was stinging her, Kutchuk danced, shedding garment after garment, until she was left divested of her clothes, standing in the middle of the rug. Afterwards she told Flaubert that she did not like to perform this dance, a remark which bears out the similar distaste of other *ghawazee* for performing nude in front of foreign men. It is left to us to imagine the nature of her particular charm. Clearly, there was something special about her.

Flaubert's encounters with Kutchuk Hanem were imbued with a melancholy which he cultivated deliberately in order to extract to the full the bitter-sweet nature of an encounter with a courtesan. She slept, snoring, with her head against his arm; an antique lamp burned on the wall beside them; just before dawn the cold woke her and, for an hour,

Previous page:
Achille Boschi. *The plate dance*. 19th century. Oil painting. Mathaf Gallery, London

she crouched before the brazier, warming herself before returning to bed and falling asleep again:

> How flattering it would be to one's pride, if at the moment of leaving you were sure that you left a memory behind, that she would think of you more than of the others who have been there, that you would remain in her heart.[43]

On his second visit to Esna, Flaubert called on Kutchuk Hanem again. He observed that she looked tired, as if she had been ill, and that this time she was wearing none of her finery (she kept her jewels and money with the sherif for fear of thieves). Knowing this would be their last meeting, he scrutinized her for a long time, committing her to memory. Flaubert used the notes from his encounters with Kutchuk Hanem for a description of Salome dancing in the short story 'Herodias'. In 'The Tale of St Anthony', the memory of Kutchuk Hanem surfaces when the Queen of Sheba tempts the saint with the offer to dance 'The Bee' for him.

Flaubert's mistress, the poet and novelist Louise Colet, was shocked when she read about Kutchuk Hanem in his travel notes. Visiting Egypt in 1864 she carefully avoided Esna, though she did make inquiries about the dancer. With some triumph she wrote that Flaubert would be interested if he could see Kutchuk Hanem now: 'She is still living — a living mummy.'

Flaubert, however, was immune to this image of the dancer, around whom he had already woven his myth, the myth of the tragic courtesan. It was a popular figure in Romantic literature and one which coincided with Flaubert's self-confessed fascination with prostitutes. The memory of Kutchuk Hanem haunted him for a long time, as can be seen from a letter to a friend in which he confessed to a melancholy desire to go back up the Nile and see her again: 'It is there that I spent a night such as one seldom spends in a lifetime, and I enjoyed it to the full.' To Louise Colet he wrote that she need not be jealous of the dancer's memory; that however much the two of them may have been thinking about Kutchuk Hanem, she was certainly not repaying the compliment. For Kutchuk Hanem, he wrote, he was just another foreigner with money.

Chapter 4

THE ARTIST'S MUSE

…an earthen hut, scarcely high enough for a woman to stand erect, in a section outside the city that was almost completely reduced to ruins. In the silence, these dancers in red and gold.

Gustave Flaubert

For the first half of the nineteenth century Paris was the centre of Orientalism. Several years before the birth of Impressionism, Hector de Callias commented on the debt owed by art to the European passion for the East:

> This passion has given [French painting] what until now has been lacking: light and the sun. What is, in effect, missing from the French Gallery at the Louvre? It is neither style in drawing nor the science of composition, nor again the harmony of colour. It is the rays of the sun.[44]

In exploring the East, artists were able to free themselves from the rules of classicism which restricted them in their own countries.

Orientalist painting glows with enthusiasm for the East, for it offered up a cornucopia of new subjects which stimulated the imagination in every way. The technical problems inherent in translating into paint the blinding white light of the desert lands, the insight to be gained from exploring the very properties of light — these were the major challenges confronting Orientalist painters. The French painter Paul Lenoir, who accompanied Gérôme to the Middle East, compared the start of their journey to the raising of a curtain. The order of the day, he wrote, was to be illusion rather than reality; it was to be a trip to a theatrical world.

Artists in flight from the gloomy, cluttered interiors and filthy air of newly industrialized Europe found in the Middle East a world of enchantment. It was a world in which the past was still considered of value, and tradition had not been brutally usurped

Facing page:
Gustavo Simoni. *The Entertainment.*
Late 19th century. Oil painting.
Mathaf Gallery, London

79

in the name of progress. Many artists admired the Arab genius for creating oases of beauty and sensual ease in the midst of an inhospitable environment.

The languor of life in the harsh heat of the East was most commonly explored by painters through themes connected with women. It must be remembered that the only women available as models, the only ones with whom artists would have had much contact, were dancers and prostitutes. The difficulty of finding models, due partly to the Islamic proscription on the reproduction of likenesses, as well as the fact that women were not allowed to expose themselves to strangers, was overcome by engaging the services of Jewish and other non-Muslim women. Most Middle Eastern women remained an unknown quantity, concealed in public by enveloping mantles and in the home behind ornate wooden *mashrabiyas*, whose carved latticework obscured the interior of a house from inquisitive eyes.

It is not surprising that artists were somewhat preoccupied by a sense of mystery in relation to women, nor that they emphasized the languorous sensuality of those with whom they did become acquainted. After all, it was through the expression of their sensuality that these women earned their living. In the eyes of many travellers, women came to epitomize the voluptuousness which characterized the East. Indeed, despite a considerable interest in other aspects of Arab culture, the life of women was to become the most popular subject of Orientalist painting.

Many critics of Orientalism subscribe to the belief that the West invented a false image of Arab women to satisfy its own particular fantasies. The myth of the mysterious veiled woman of the East could not, however, have been created had women not had a symbolic importance in the eyes of their own men. The concealment of women in the harem and behind enveloping veils as well as their exclusion from public life indicate how great this symbolic value was, and still is today.

'Harem' is derived from the Semitic root *hrm*, which carries connotations of prohibition and exclusion. The harem may have come into being as a result of settlement in towns, as a protective device for women against outsiders, although we do not

Previous page:
Otto Pilny. *A dance at sunset.*
Mid-19th century. Oil painting.
Sotheby's, London

know for certain when it was first instituted. Arab poetry, however, indicates that it was already in existence at the time of the first Caliphate, which followed the death of the Prophet Muhammad in AD 632.

Islam has drawn heavily on the two male-centred faiths which preceded it in the Middle East. As we have seen, these religions shared a profound distrust and fear of women, due largely to what was considered their dangerous sexuality. There has never been a true reconciliation with the feminine in the Arab world. There, women are seen as a potentially disruptive force, due to the assumption that men are unable to resist their powerful lure. The word for 'chaos' in Arabic is the same as that used to describe a beautiful woman, *fitna*, a word which carries all the connotations of the *femme fatale*.[45] The solution to the problem of what is seen by Muslim men as woman's disruptive sexual power is threefold: to define her sphere of influence as the home; to confine her presence to the harem, where children are reared and the daily business of the household is carried out; and to enforce the use of the veil.

Islam has always had its greatest influence among settled communities. In villages and among the nomadic bedouin it has had to accommodate pre-existing traditions which evolved in response to the practical problems of desert life. If an incoming faith does not offer solutions to the problem of survival in a desert environment, it stands little chance of making a deep impression. Among bedouin women veiling is a custom which hinders the practical business of everyday work, and is not observed; it is often the men who cover their faces, to protect themselves from the wind and sand on their journeys into the desert.

Orientalist painters discovered in the veil the perfect metaphor for the unknown, and used it to symbolize the hidden, tantalizing nature of Middle Eastern women. As the French painter Renoir commented, Arab women knew the value of concealment and were adept at exploiting it; an eye half glimpsed through a veil was particularly alluring. Europe's expectations of Middle Eastern women were influenced by the work of another French painter Ingres, although he did not travel in the East

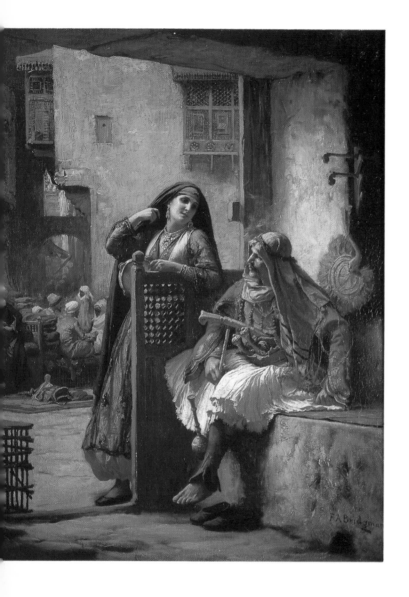

Frederick Arthur Bridgman. *A musician taking time off between performances*. 19th century. Oil painting. Private collection

himself. His knowledge, sifted through the experience of others, derived from literature such as the travel letters of Lady Mary Wortley Montagu, who lived for several months in Constantinople in 1717. Ingres' 'Turkish Bath' was inspired by Lady Mary's description of a *hammam* (public bath) in Adrianople, 'the women's coffee-house' as she called it. Here all the latest gossip was exchanged and the women spent the day lying on richly worked rugs, eating and drinking, embroidering and having their hair braided by slaves. Sometimes a company of dancers and female musicians was brought in to add to the general pleasure of the occasion:

> Nothing could be more artful or more proper to raise certain ideas. The tunes so soft! The motions so languishing! Accompanied with pauses and dying eyes; half falling back and then recovering themselves in so artful a manner that, I am very positive, the coldest and most rigid prude on earth could not have looked upon them without thinking of something not to be spoken of.[46]

Ingres read Lady Mary's letters while he was working on his 'Turkish Bath'. It is an unlikely scene that he conjures up, a sea of plump, reclining women crowded in so closely that we have the impression of bodies piled on top of each other. Despite Lady Mary's comment that she did not see a single wanton or immodest look between the women, some of Ingres' bathers adopt poses which are highly suggestive.

Of course, male painters did not see the inside of either the harem or the *hammam*. They had to rely on women's reports and their own fantasies in the creation of such interiors, and it is often the fantasy which triumphs. On a visit to a Turkish *hammam* in 1839, the English traveller Julia Pardoe mentions that the women were not nude but were dressed in fine lawn blouses saturated with vapour. Their black slaves, on the other hand, were naked from the waist up.

Orientalist paintings of women at their toilette are said to have satisfied a market for erotic nudes, but the 'Turkish Bath' is so overworked, so surfeited with flesh, that it has become a parody. In the background, scarcely discernible in the shadows, a woman dances on her toes like a ballerina. Paintings of dancers often show them performing in the manner of an artist's own country. Thus the dancer in Francesco Coleman's 'Before the Performance', standing hands on hips, waiting to begin, not only has the look of a temperamental Latin signorina but seems as if she is about to launch into a wild fandango. Nor do her face and skin tones suggest the Middle East, but then, this is a common feature of the genre.

It has been suggested that depicting a woman with the fair complexion of a European 'brought her closer to Western standards of beauty'. For hundreds of years fair skin has been considered a sign of beauty in the East, and for the same reason as in the West: it was a reflection of social position.

Rodriguez Etchart. *A private entertainment*. Mid-19th century. Oil painting. Mathaf Gallery, London

A woman who worked out in the fields all day was too busy to make sure her face was protected from the elements. In Ottoman Turkey Circassian women were especially prized for their beauty, due chiefly to their fair colouring, and most of those bought in the slave markets of Constantinople were destined for the sultan's harem at Topkapi. Gérôme was one painter who prided himself on being able to distinguish the facial characteristics of Turks, Circassians and Egyptians. Like other painters he used daguerrotypes as a quick method of recording a scene. His 'Dance of the Almeh' is a masterly evocation of an Egyptian woman entertaining a group of Turkish mercenaries.

The picture is also an accurate representation of *baladi*: the dancer's stance is correct in every detail, from the position of her lifted arms and the manner of holding her finger cymbals to the hint of gold spangles in her hair. Even the angle of her curved head is correct. She looks as if she is describing a circle with her upraised hip, using her other leg as the pivot while she slowly wheels around. Gérôme has captured perfectly the earthiness of *baladi*, whose centre of gravity is low in the hips, a feature not observed by all artists. Some dancers in Orientalist paintings look as if they are about to soar into space, their centre of movement higher up, in the solar plexus, as in Western ballet.

In Gérôme's painting the soldiers' gravity and reserve lend the scene a sombre quality; their faces are tense and apprehensive, and only the African is wholeheartedly enjoying himself. The audience reacts differently in Gaston Saintpierre's 'Algerian Wedding'. Here the women are entertaining each other in the courtyard of the house, and their delight and involvement in the performance are evident. They watch with the kind of appreciative concentration which anyone who has been present at such an occasion would instantly recognize.

Middle Eastern women sometimes remark that they are the ones who really appreciate the dance, and it is true that men and women enjoy it for different reasons. Women are quick to recognize a well-executed or difficult movement and encourage a good dancer with the *zhagareet*, and by clapping in time to the music, as can be seen in Saintpierre's portrait. Delacroix's 'Jewish Wedding in Morocco'

Facing page:
Gaston Saintpierre. *Women's wedding party in Algeria.* 1870s. Oil painting. Private collection

Etienne Dinet. *A moonlight dance on the terrace*. 1916. Oil painting. Private collection

Previous page:
Jean-Léon Gérôme. *Dance of the almeh*. c.1875. Oil painting. Dayton Art Institute, Ohio

shows the women peering over the banisters of an upstairs balcony in order to catch a glimpse of the troupe which has been brought in to entertain the men.

One of the charges constantly levelled against the Orientalist portrayal of women is that artists were voyeurs who used the dance as a symbol of Eastern 'exhibitionism'. Rana Kabbani writes:

> [The dance] often became a trope for the Orient's abandon, for it seemed to be a dramatically different mode of dancing from its Western counterpart. It was not a social expression only, since the woman, scantily clad as she was pictured, was there to please the onlooker, who did not participate but watched.[47]

She adds in a footnote, 'Although the dance in European literature also has sexual undertones, the man in it is active participant rather than voyeur.'

It is impossible to compare European dance with its Arabic counterpart, for the two stem from a radically different use of the body, as well as a different concept of 'performer' and 'spectator'. The above comments beg the question, what artist is not a voyeur — in other words, an observer, looking from the outside in? Similarly, what entertainer is not performing to please his or her audience? To delight the eye of the onlooker — or, as Kabbani would have it, the voyeur — is the chief *raison d'être* of the professional dancer. Nor can social dance be put in the same category as its theatrical counterpart, as if both shared a similar motivation.

To imply that if men were involved in the dancing the exercise would be more justifiable is to deny the very nature of *baladi* and the tradition out of which it has grown. Both male and female critics of Orientalism often seem uncomfortable when faced with the subject and are not sure how to deal with it. Kabbani vilifies both artist and onlooker (she assumes the audience is exclusively male) for even enjoying a dance performance. Nor is it the case that Orientalist painters showed 'scantily clad' dancers. On the contrary, unlike the numerous portraits of women in the *hammam*, dancers are generally shown splendidly attired.

This kind of criticism denies the artist's autonomy and seeks to replace it with a formula dictated by the critic's own social ideals. Art is not documentary reportage; the creation of any work is a selective, imaginative process. All artists take what they need in order to produce a successful work of art; their aim is rarely a faithful representation of the scene which originally inspired a painting or piece of writing. On the whole, portraits of dancers avoid the stereotypes evident in scenes of the harem and *hammam*. Performers are shown dressed in all their finery, active and proud, full of energy and grace. The pleasure of the occasion is what shines through in the eyes of both spectators and performers. The dancers are not portrayed as mysterious; they look as if they are enjoying themselves as much as their audience.

In the nineteenth century Europeans were looking back to the days before the coming of industrialism and its attendant evils. Liberty, both at home and abroad, was a subject of concern throughout Western Europe. The Greek revolt against Ottoman power became a celebrated cause, while in England it was the time of the factory reform movement and the campaign against slavery — an institution which flourished in both East and West, and survived into the twentieth century in the East.

Throughout Europe and America people were in revolt against cruelty and barbarism and many had a dual attitude towards Middle Eastern life: a reaction against evils which the West itself was combating at the time, and admiration for the liberty and nobility they saw in the life of the desert bedouin. Carl Jung wrote that we have an unconscious knowledge that the process of civilization has robbed us of our vital self, and it has now become a truism that we tend to make either a god or a devil out of what our society most lacks and needs. The East was attractive partly because it had apparently retained the best of a more primitive life which the West had suppressed and gone on to despise.

After their experience of the Arab world, a number of artists and travellers found that they could no longer endure the life offered them by their own society, and took the difficult step of exile. The French painter Etienne Dinet was among them. Dinet first visited Algeria in 1884. After that he

Etienne Dinet. *A dancer of the Ouled Nail.* 1890. Gouache. Private collection

Eugène Delacroix. *Jewish wedding in Morocco*. c. 1837. Oil painting. Louvre Museum, Paris

spent every summer there, painting in the south, and gradually became more and more involved with the country and its people until, in 1904, he went to live there permanently. Towards the end of his life he became a convert to Islam and went on the pilgrimage to Mecca. On his death, the street where he had lived in Bou Saada ('place of happiness') was named after him.

Dinet is known for his life-long study of the women of the Ouled Nail, a tribe who lived in the stone desert of the Sahara and could be found in settlements between Biskra and Laghouat. The women grew up learning to dance from infancy, and when they were about 12 years old they left home and made their way to the oases to begin a new life. They lived with an older woman who took on the role of housekeeper, and travelled from oasis to oasis, entertaining in the cafés and combining the profession of dancer and prostitute. When they had earned enough money for their dowry they stopped working and married, after which they carried on the tradition of their tribe by teaching their daughters to dance.

Like *ghawazee*, 'Ouled Nail' came to be used as a term for dancers in general, irrespective of their particular tribe. In the early years after the French occupation of Algeria in 1830, large numbers of French soldiers were billeted in the area around Biskra, with the result that the town developed into a centre of commerce and entertainment. By the late nineteenth century it had become a setting-off point for Saharan travel and a place where tourists could sit in the cafés and be entertained by the Ouled Nail.

Many dances of the Maghreb are performed in a group, with women successively stepping forward to perform a solo or duet while the rest of the group maintains a chanting, hand-clapping accompaniment. This type of dance expresses daily life and work, as well as individual encounters between people. It is especially concerned with the rituals of nature. The feet shuffle back and forth, pressing the ground and beating the soil to awaken the earth spirits, movements symbolic of penetration and fertility. Gestures of the hands express a desire to create a link between heaven and earth, the individual and the community, the mortal and the immortal. With elaborate, fluttering hands a dancer indicates her audience, touching her breast in greeting — 'I take you to my heart' — while beneath her heavy costume her hips and stomach rhythmically rise and fall.

The dance of the Ouled Nail, with its strong black African influence, its ritual nature and repetitive movements, was a style in which Western visitors found little to attract them. Even the solo dance, which the women launch with shrill cries of the *zhagareet*, was compared unfavourably to *baladi*, whose fluidity and grace the foreigners could more readily appreciate. One traveller remarked:

> Unlike the Egyptian dancers, who specialize in soft, undulating, serpentine movements of the abdominal muscles, the Ouled Nail pride themselves in being able to make their belly pulsate violently and in syncopation to the music.[48]

American dancer Ted Shawn noted with distaste how the women moved each breast in turn. He went on to say:

> It is not a suggestive dance, for the simple reason that it leaves nothing to the imagination, and because of this unashamed animality, revolts the average white tourist to the point of being unable to admire the phenomenal mastery these women have of parts of the body over which we have no voluntary control at all.[49]

Western interest in the Ouled Nail focused largely on their physical appearance. 'An exhibition of mummies or relics', noted one French anthropologist with wonder, remarking on the women's henna'ed hair, their eyebrows pencilled in to meet over the bridge of the nose and their apparently ill-matched layers of clothing. This costume consisted of embroidered, smock-like dresses worn one on top of the other, with open, bell-like sleeves either left hanging or gathered in at the wrist. Over these dresses was worn a *haik*, a length of woollen or cotton cloth, draped around the body and secured at the shoulder with a *bezima*, an outsize clasp which sometimes had chains and talismans to ward off evil spirits attached to it. Shawn, who saw the Ouled

Etienne Dinet. *Bedouin dancers of Algeria*. 1896. Oil painting. Private collection

Nail in the 1920s, commented that these *bezimas* were often the size of pancake-turners. He added that the women's jewellery covered them like chainmail and that, to protect themselves from thieves, they wore huge bracelets, 'really murderous-looking objects' with studs and spikes an inch or two long projecting from them. The women wore their waist-length hair braided with wool and twined round their ears, where it was held in place with strips of material. Some of them wore tiaras inlaid with coral, turquoise and enamel, and earrings so large they had to be hung on ribbons of fabric and tied over the head.

A number of painters sought to capture the extravagance of the women's dress by exaggerating it. The French painter Georges Clairins, for whom the Ouled Nail were a favourite theme, portrays them as Amazons, magnifying the size of their headdresses and positioning them against the walls of courtyards in the full glare of the sun, a cigarette casually dangling between their fingers. Their flimsy white dresses are as fine and delicate as those of any aristocratic Frenchwoman, and are a far cry from the costume which Shawn found dirty, tatty and torn.

It has been remarked that Orientalist painters elaborated on the strangeness of their subjects. While this is true to some extent, it is not always the case that the East was portrayed as picturesque and odd. Many painters valued the strangeness of the East and did not fall into the trap of perceiving Oriental life merely as odd. They sought to understand the unfamiliar customs of the East, and recorded them in paintings which have become the reliquaries of a vanished culture. Some were aware that the very traditions which attracted them were in the process of dying out, and considered it their task to record them for the sake of future generations. The English artist William Holman Hunt, visiting Jerusalem in 1855, wrote, 'I cannot believe that Art should let such beautiful things pass as are in this age passing for good in the East without exertion to chronicle them for the future.' It could be dangerous work. Holman Hunt painted with a rifle by his side as protection against wild animals and hostile bedouin, while Delacroix, visiting North Africa in 1832, was spat at and cursed and had to be escorted by soldiers every time he went out.

Critics of Orientalism tend to belittle the West's desire to chronicle the traditions of Middle Eastern life. One contemporary writer has commented on the West's 'addiction to knowledge' as though the spirit of inquiry were a sickness, as well as a plot aimed at intellectual (hence actual) control. This implied praise of ignorance shows how far such critics are from grasping the misunderstanding in this nineteenth-century collision between cultures. Both East and West have benefited from the historical and anthropological studies made during the nineteenth century. And without this legacy we would have little detailed knowledge of Arabic dance in the past.

Muhammad Racim was one Arab artist who sought to record the vanishing customs and dress of his native city, Algiers, for the benefit of posterity. His miniatures of dancers entertaining at private gatherings show them posing decorously to show off their finery, the Turkish costume of Algeria in the 1830s. Paintings of the dancers appeared less frequently as the art of photography developed and the women began appearing in person in the West, where they came to entertain at the great trade fairs.

Most lengthy descriptions of them were written in the middle and latter part of the nineteenth century. Much of the writing was the work of men, who rarely looked beyond the performance element of their lives. It was left to a woman writer to give us a glimpse of the human being beneath the professional charmer. The French writer Colette spent several years as a dance-mime artist in turn-of-the-century Paris. Colette's fiction explores the lives of women and is imbued with an appreciation and love of the sensual in all its guises. Her fine-spun portraits of women living on the margins of society, dependent for survival on their beauty and charm, are shot through with an acute psychological understanding of her subject.

During a performance tour of Algeria Colette was taken one night to visit an Ouled Nail woman in her home:

> The guide halted before a barely visible door and struck it with his staff. No one came, and

A dancer of the cafés. 1914. Tinted photograph. *Arabesque* collection, New York

we could hear only the faint sounds of a party in a distant house,... a rustling of nearby palms and the pattering of sand carried by the night wind, shifting and raining finely against the walls.

The guide banged louder, using the tip of his staff, and a ray of light shone through the cautiously opening door. A clash of bracelets, necklaces and earrings came towards us; the reflection from the sand showed us the gleam of eyes and teeth and jewels dangling around the face. Our guide exchanged a few sentences with the indistinctly seen woman. She was obviously protesting vigorously and he, brusquely insisting. At last she moved back and invited us to enter.[50]

The woman, Yasmina, having agreed to entertain the group, immediately slipped into her professional manner, offering tea and making her visitors comfortable. Having satisfied the formalities, she called in a couple of musicians from outside and proceeded to dance:

> Like all the Ouled Nail she danced using her arms and hands, her feet merely brushing the floor, as if on hot paving. When she danced she also used her flanks and the muscles of her vigorous belly. Then she stopped for a moment's rest, using the interval to undo her bodice, shirt and chemise — for the guide insisted that she dance nude. She returned to the middle of the room between us and the two musicians, who had now turned their backs... She danced the same dances, knowing no others. But because of her nudity she no longer smiled but turned her gaze away from us and refused any longer to meet our eyes. She looked away and above our heads, full of a regal gravity and disdain, seeking the distant, invisible desert.[51]

Colette's is one of the few descriptions of an Ouled Nail dancer by a woman. It is also the most poignant, concentrating on Yasmina's feelings rather than her dance, which merits only a few lines. It tells us more about the realities of life for Yasmina and her fellow

Previous page:
Muhammad Racim. *Algerian scarf dance*. c.1830. Miniature. Private collection

dancers than all the other accounts of these women combined.

The Ouled Nail, resplendent in their headdresses and chainmail of jewellery, and the *ghawazee*, dancing in dark cafés, eagerly sought after and at the same time despised, have slipped into the past largely unknown to us by name. Yet through their arresting dance they live on, in travel writing, short stories and paintings, a memory which endures through the alchemy of art.

DANCERS FROM THE EAST

How strange did this dance seem to us; but is it not probable that our waltz would seem equally strange to these dusky women of Egypt?

F.W. Putnam, *Portrait Types of the Midway Plaisance*

When a dance is taken out of its cultural context and served up as a theatrical spectacle in the outside world it necessarily changes. The ways in which it does so are largely to do with satisfying the expectations of its new-found audience, who come to see it armed with their own unconscious tastes and prejudices. Out of place in its new setting, presented as a brief interlude, a variety act among others, it is often misunderstood and perceived merely as an oddity.

In 1851 London's Crystal Palace was built to house an exhibition of world culture and new developments in science and technology. Commerce and industry, dress and food, art and entertainment were represented in mock-up towns and villages from all over the world. The Crystal Palace Exhibition was exported to New York in 1853, and two years later a similar venture was held in Paris, the first of a series of expositions held there at eleven-year intervals until 1900.

This type of trade fair mushroomed throughout the cities of the West in the remaining years of the century. For many of the general public, the greatest attraction of these fairs was the entertainment they offered. The year 1893 saw the Great Columbia Exposition in Chicago. Its entertainment section, the Midway Plaisance, boasted a Moorish palace, Turkish and Persian theatres and a Cairo street, complete with troupes of indigenous entertainers. The Egyptian dancing, performed by Fahreda Mahzar (who hailed from Syria), proved the sensation of the fair. Tickets to see her cost between 20 and 75 cents, depending on location, as opposed to a 25 cent flat rate to see her rivals. Yet the Cairo street boasted capacity audiences while its neighbours drew only a handful of customers.

A dancer of the fellahin. 1890s. Tinted photograph. Private collection

101

Fahreda Mahzar came to be known as Little Egypt. Sol Bloom, the son of poor immigrants and a future congressman who was responsible for the entertainments concessions on the Midway Plaisance, later denied in his autobiography that he had ever had anything to do with a female dancer known familiarly as Little Egypt. Perhaps his exalted status, plus the notoriety which had by then become attached to her name, dissuaded him from claiming any acquaintance. For Little Egypt became the most talked-of attraction of the fair. According to the *New York Herald Tribune*, 'She drew more attention than the seventy-ton telescope or the six-block-long Manufactures and Liberal Arts Building.'

Some of the attention was unwelcome. The fair's Board of Lady Managers demanded that future exhibitions be restricted 'within the limits of stage propriety as recognized in this country'. It was a complaint echoed by others, yet Little Egypt was not typical of all the dancers who performed at the fair. Commemorative photos indicate that traditional folk dances were just as much a feature of these Orient Shows. F.W. Putnam, who produced a commemorative book of portraits featuring the dancers, commented of the Algerian troupe that they were agile and far more graceful than the pirouetting of a première, and wore far more clothes than the ballerinas of the Paris Opéra.

Others were of a different opinion. A souvenir booklet of the fair comments that, 'though the dancers were lithe as panthers and should have been capable of graceful movements, their dancing can hardly be considered a dance so much as a contortion'.[52] Julia Ward Howe, an early American feminist, reported a performance she saw as being 'simply horrid, no touch of grace about it, only the most deforming movement of the whole abdominal and lumbar region'. The dance — a potentially liberating experience — confronted her with her prejudices, as it has confronted Western women ever since. Like many, she did not rise to the challenge but preferred to acquiesce with patriarchal values concerning sensual expression and the female body.

During the last days of the fair farewell poems to the dancers appeared in the press, yet we find none dedicated to Little Egypt, though there were

eulogies to Zareefa the bedouin dancer, Jamelee from Syria and, Rosa from the Turkish theatre. However, it was Little Egypt who inspired a host of imitators. Meanwhile other dancers who had appeared at the fair returned home with the $500 they had each received for their six-month sojourn in Chicago. It was an enormous sum of money for a dancer in those days and it prompted others to set out for Europe and America in search of fame and fortune.

From 1893 onwards burlesque shows throughout America presented the attractions of dancers calling themselves Little Egypt, some American, others not, who performed in ways Fahreda Mahzar had never done. She herself went on to marry a Greek restaurateur and continued performing in an increasingly conservative manner, while her imitators grew bolder and more outrageous. She often had occasion to protest vigorously at the host of Little Egypts whose lewd acts were attributed to her, and in 1937, with a law suit pending against one of them, she died of a heart attack. Legends abound concerning the effect she had on her audience. The American writer Mark Twain is even said to have had a heart attack when he saw her dance. But which Little Egypt did he see?

Leichenstein and Harari. *Entertainers from the East*. 1880s. Postcard. Private collection

At the Columbia Exposition Fahreda Mahzar danced to the sound of flutes and drums. One report noted that, as part of her act, she lay down, placed two partially filled glasses on her stomach and made them clink together in time to the music. Sometimes she balanced a candlestick on her head. Occasionally she appeared minus shoes and stockings and tucked her voluminous skirt above her left knee, exposing her long white cotton underwear.

It was an era when men used to stare and whisper as women climbed the steps of the new-fangled trolley cars, revealing a few inches of cotton-stockinged ankle. Years later, a burlesque entertainer of that time wrote:

> It's amusing now to recall, and perhaps incredible, but seeing a woman's ankle in those days was a novelty. Men would stand on the street corner and wait and watch for girls to cross the street so they could see them raise their skirts. A rainy day would be a rich harvest.[53]

In such a climate of sexual repression and obsession, it is hardly surprising that Arabic dance was considered shocking.

A thirty-second film entitled variously *Danse du Ventre* and *Passion Dance* was made in 1896, featuring the American dancer Dolorita. This flickering black-and-white record shows a fleshy woman in voluminous low-slung pantaloons, her breasts barely concealed beneath a fine lawn chemise and a bodice bursting at the seams. Straddling the stage, she gyrates wildly, her body a mass of shaking, pulsating flesh. With a smile of singular sweetness she sinks to her knees, thrusting her pelvis at the camera.

Shown in slot machines on the boardwalk of Atlantic City, it held the record in peep-show popularity until a public watchdog, observing the queues lining up to see it, took a look for himself and complained to the authorities. The film was subsequently withdrawn. The main objection to it was the boldness of its pelvic movements. *Danse du Ventre* and another short, *Fatima's Dance*, recorded at Coney Island during the same period, were among the first films to be censored in the

'Fatima's Dance'. c.1896. Film still. Museum of Modern Art, New York

history of the cinema. They were shown with black or white bars painted across every frame, with the result that the head is the only part of the body which can be clearly seen.

The uncensored version of *Fatima's Dance* shows a woman who, to judge from her technique, could well be from the Middle East. She wears a striped skirt with necklaces of dangling coins, a puff-sleeved striped bodice, high-heeled shoes and a decorous little pillbox hat perched on her hair. As she turns around we can glimpse the bobbles on her garters just below the knees which hold up her white stockings. Playing finger cymbals throughout the dance, she first sets up a vigorous shaking of the hips, gives a little jump to one side, crossing one foot in front of the other, then a similar jump to the other side. A shoulder shimmy follows, then a gliding, undulating walk emphasizing a forward tilting of the hips, with one hand held aloft, the other hidden behind her back. This film not only shows us the form of the dance at the end of the nineteenth century; it corresponds with written accounts from an earlier era. It confirms a continuity of style and shows how little the dance has changed, even down to the present day.

The physical appearance of the dancers who appeared at the world fairs was often met with a combination of distaste and disappointment:

> Their kinky hair, dirty butter complexions, bad features, stained teeth, and tendency to *embonpoint* are dreadfully disillusioning, their voices are of a timbre that would drive an American cat in disgrace from any well-regulated neighbourhood.[54]

The problem was that people's expectations had been fuelled by the image of Oriental dancing offered by Western art and literature. Oriental women were supposedly characterized by their mystery, languor and veiled beauty. The mere mortals who came West with their musicians in search of work did not dress in the flowing costumes of Orientalist painting. Western influence on their everyday dress is reflected in the shortened skirts, stockings and shoes which they wore in commemorative photos of the exhibitions. The women's *embonpoint*, or

Hammersmitt. *One of the earliest known studio portraits of a dancer, Egypt.* 1870s. Photograph. Private collection

Studio portrait of Egyptian entertainers. 1890s. Photograph. Private collection

Arnaud. *Studio portrait.* 1880s. Photograph. Private collection

fleshiness, considered beautiful in their own countries, was not so highly regarded in the West. Having been a source of fantasy for years, when they finally appeared in person they were greeted with some confusion.

Performers of *baladi* found their dance tagged with a variety of names, including *danse du ventre* (belly dance) and *hoochie koochie* (after the Kooch dancers of India). The latter indicates a further element of confusion. Turkey, Egypt, Syria, Persia and India were all thrown into the same spicy casserole labelled Oriental. It did not matter which country an entertainer hailed from; she was still expected to produce the kind of performance celebrated in the numerous accounts of Egyptian *baladi.*

Photography provided an added element of anticipation. From the 1840s photos of dancers had been appearing in the form of picture postcards, posed shots often produced in a studio setting, using models who may or may not have been dancers in real life. Many of these early studios belonged to Europeans, the best known among them being the Bonfils brothers, based in Beirut, and Lehnet and Landrock in Cairo. Most pictures were produced expressly for a Western market and show the women in unlikely poses. A bare-breasted girl leans against a doorway, squinting into the sunlight, holding a tambourine over her head. Or she reclines on a couch playing the *oud* (Arab lute), her dress unfastened at the shoulders, leaving her upper torso bare. Needless to say, the captions on these postcards are similarly contrived. The same woman can be seen posing in different national costumes in a number of studies, portraying an inhabitant of any one of several Arab countries.

The women were generally paid a small sum for posing and often look uneasy, if not downright bored, for photography was a laborious process in its infancy. Subjects were required to stand perfectly motionless for anything up to two minutes. Standing beside the potted palms of a Beirut studio, the tense expression on their faces may also reflect an ambivalent attitude towards being captured on film at all, for in many countries it was (and still is) believed that to take someone's likeness robs them of their soul.

Zanjaki. *Egyptian musician wearing a traditional veil*. 1880s. Photograph. Private collection

Francis Bedford. *Dancer*. 1880s. Photograph. Private collection

However, there is also an element of humour in some of these portraits. One in particular, a picture of a world fair dancer, shows a tired-looking woman, feet squarely planted, hand on hip, one arm raised above her head, holding a set of brass finger cymbals. She looks as if she has seen it all before and found none of it pleasing. A look of utter boredom, an absence of any attempt at a graceful pose are compounded by the expression in her eyes, as if to say, 'Hurry up, can't you, my arm's about to drop off!' In another study a woman looks into the camera with contempt. We have already seen her in several pictures pretending to be a musician; this time she is pretending to be a singer.

In contrast to these posed shots are the studies of Ouled Nail dancers taken in Bou Saada and published in the *National Geographic Magazine* in January 1914. One of them shows a fiercely proud figure, a cigarette dangling out of the corner of her mouth, glaring at the camera with a look that could

kill. She seems well able to deal with anyone who is foolish enough to try and get on the wrong side of her.

It has been suggested that these women, like butterflies pinned on cork, were victims of the photographer, who deprived them of their dignity as human beings. However, it is far more the case that they were victims of their own society. Through an accident of birth, through nationality (often they were from minority communities), through sudden misfortune or a failed marriage, they earned their living in a culture which despised and distrusted any woman who did not live under the jurisdiction of a husband or other male relative.

The majority of dancers who came to work in the world fairs and cabarets of Europe and America did not record their feelings and thoughts on the matter. So it is with interest that we turn to one who did. Armen Ohanian was in every way unlike her contemporaries in the early years of the twentieth century. She was a rare phenomenon of the time: a well-educated girl of prosperous family who became a professional dancer. Nor did she perform in the same milieu as the others — but sought a setting other than cafés and sideshows in which to perform. Her abiding ambition was to gain respect for her art in the eyes of the world for, from an early age, she was familiar with the contempt in which dancers were held. She remembered, as a young bride, being taken by her husband's uncle to a bazaar in Tehran where she watched a child dancing with a tambourine. The child's hair was dishevelled, her face old beyond her years, full of weariness and heartache, and when she held out her tambourine for payment, the jeering crowd rewarded her with pebbles and rotten eggs. Horrified, Armen begged her uncle to take her away. He agreed, saying, 'Why should we look at this lost girl? There is nothing in the world more wicked than a dancer.'

Armen Ohanian's autobiography is a rare account from this period of an 'Oriental' dancer's life written from the inside. It is full of insight into the minutiae of a woman's life in the Middle East and the public response to those of her calling. Originally from Armenia, on her father's death Armen was sent to Persia, where a marriage had been contracted for her. The failure of this marriage presented her with

108

two options: either to return to her ex-husband's family or, in her own words, to cast herself to the four winds and seek her way in the world. Determined to put an unhappy past behind her, she turned to her childhood love of dance, perhaps as much from a lack of any other alternative as from a burning desire for recognition, although this came later.

Early experiences performing in Egypt led to a contract to appear in Europe. The early years of this century found her in Paris, at that time the cultural capital of the West, where she became the fashion of the moment. Writer Anatole France was sufficient of an admirer to write a fulsome introduction to her first book of memoirs, *The Dancer of Shamahka*, which was translated into a rather flowery English. She followed it up with a second, in many ways more interesting book, *Les Rires d'une Charmeuse de Serpents* (The Laughter of a Snake-Charmer). From the pages of these books emerges the picture of a melancholy, somewhat humourless woman of passionate conviction.

Much of her first volume of memoirs is taken up with the story of her failed marriage. From the moment Armen arrived at the home of her betrothed she was plagued by ill omens. A lamb was slaughtered at her feet as a mark of welcome, but its blood refused to flow towards her, to the horror of her future mother-in-law.

Homesickness and the strain of adapting to an unaccustomed lifestyle began to tell on her. The forty days she spent preparing for her duties as a wife left her intimidated and nervous of shadows. When she fell prey to terrifying nightmares from which she awoke screaming in the middle of the night, holy men were called in. They told her she was possessed by evil spirits. Talismans to ward off these spirits were hung round her neck and she was made to dance through the streets to the tombs of the saints, in a trance ritual designed to dispel the evil surrounding her. 'The spirits, made wretched by my rapid movements, and the sharp sounds of the cymbals, would leave me, and when they sought to return, the talismans would prevent them.' However, the ceremony failed to work and by the day of her wedding Armen was in a state of nervous exhaustion.

Studio portrait entitled 'Two Arab women and their servant'. 1890s.
Postcard. Private collection

Facing page:
A young girl of the Ouled Nail. 1914.
Photograph. *National Geographic Magazine*

Ouled Nail dancer. 1914. Photograph.
National Geographic Magazine

A woman of the Ouled Nail. 1914.
Photograph. *National Geographic Magazine*

Musician holding a reque. 1890s.
Postcard. Private collection

On her wedding night she waited for her husband in her room. As a mark of respect she decided not to touch the food and drink which had been laid out for the two of them until he arrived. Waiting for him, she fell asleep beside the brazier, jerking awake as the lamp flickered and went out. As she watched the fire slowly cover itself with ashes, she felt a chill of misgiving creep into her heart.

Following Armen's wedding night, in time-honoured tradition, the blood-stained sheets were taken from the bed and hung out of the window as a proof of her virginity:

> These customs inspired in me a fierce aversion to marriage, an aversion which became physical. My rejected husband did not understand the reason. Feeling himself frozen out, he adopted a proud air, while the older members of the family were outraged. I no longer spoke to them. I never forgave them that display of the nuptial sheets.[55]

Her husband consoled himself in the arms of 'less chaste but more welcoming women' and Armen attempted suicide. Convalescing in hospital from the bullet wound, she met a woman who introduced herself as the Queen of the Crowns, a relative of the Shah, who invited Armen to go and live with her in her palace. There, one afternoon, she saw a performance by a group of *mutrubes* (courtesan-dancers). Rugs and cushions were brought out and spread on the ground; wine, sorbets, dishes of fruit, musical instruments and opium pipes were laid out on the rugs and strewn with freshly cut rose petals. Armen and her hostess decided to watch the entertainment in secret from behind the windows of their basement rooms which overlooked the garden.

At last it was evening and the *mutrubes* arrived. They were accompanied by a woman in her forties who had retired from the profession and whose job it was to teach the younger *mutrubes*:

> the science of pleasing the eye, of dancing, being open-hearted, reciting beautiful poems, scattering through their conversation jewels of proverbs; how to flatter shy wooers, to be bold with bold men, to be grave in the evening and to blossom into flowers of love in the dawn.

There was an adolescent girl among them who, clad in a transparent white robe tied at the hips with a scarlet sash, danced 'a poem of the awakening of the lotus to the sunshine, sung by little quiverings of the body'. The older woman then sang some melancholy fragments of old poems and legends. After she and the young girl had retired into the house, the *mutrubes* removed their outer garments and danced for the men in their long-sleeved silken tunics embroidered with gold:

> The eyes of the princes were locked upon the palpitating throats and slender arms of the dancers. Bending forward to the ground, the girls, like charming serpents, slid their bodies along the carpets to the rhythm of the slow music, laughing, almost reaching the arms held out to them, then retreating again when an eager touch would have broken the rhythm of the dance.[56]

This party compounded Armen's growing restlessness and she decided to relinquish her life of luxurious indolence. She tells us that, ever since her childhood when she taught herself to dance, she had been fascinated by the old dances of her native land. Now she decided to tread the path of a professional performer. Various adventures led to an invitation to dance for an Egyptian pasha.

In Cairo she presented herself at the palace, where she entertained the pasha's wife who was not allowed to attend Armen's performance later that night due to the presence of Europeans:

> In respectful Asiatic manner my musicians had turned their backs upon the Khediva, which obliged me to follow with my dance the breezes of their inspiration, a task indeed awkward for an Asiatic dancer, whose gestures are always followed by the music and not controlled by it.[57]

That night, Armen performed for a motley gathering which included a number of European 'princesses' married to Middle Eastern men. She discovered that these princesses were originally 'all singers in the European cabarets of Morocco and Algiers before their rise to thrones' and the acquisition of Muslim husbands.

Turkish dancer. 1890s. Postcard.
Private collection

111

An Armenian Khan proceeded to lecture her on the wicked ways of the world: ' "Your feet are set upon a downward path, my daughter," he sighed. "You will soon be changed from an honest woman to an artist. Your fall is inevitable." ' This fall, he said, would come from a love of gain, and when Armen denied that she would ever succumb to the temptation for wealth and luxury he insisted that, in that case, she would find herself in an even worse position, of abject poverty. Having, so he thought, thoroughly frightened her, he proceeded to proposition her himself, rather than leave it to someone else.

Disillusioned with Egypt, Armen was casting about for possibilities when she was offered a contract to appear in the English music hall:

> To be a star! How beautiful! But my very soul shuddered at that word 'artist'. Under that name, in the East, one spoke of the unfortunate women brought from the West by the slave merchants. No one remembered ever having seen a performance given by these artists, because, on the very day of their arrival, they were bought for a sum of gold and disappeared into private harems.[58]

After much deliberation Armen signed the contract, not understanding a word of it:

> From that moment I became independent, that is to say, thrown to the mercy of events. Independence. Proud word, created to reduce the proudest to slavery.

It is at this point that the first volume of her memoirs ends.

We next find her as the darling of Parisian society, 'the little Persian', and an ironic note begins to creep into her recollections. The available milieux could not hope to satisfy her craving to be taken seriously as an artist. Dancing in the salons of the wealthy might provide her with a living, but only as a curiosity.

> In the salons a good time was still being had. During the pre-war frenzy they paid their dolls

handsomely. There 'the little Persian' was a novelty, with her silent manner and her smile which was considered 'Leonardesque' and which hid the sadness in her eyes.[59]

She gives us an amusing account of a typical night entertaining the Parisian élite. Her services were engaged by an American sewing-machine manufacturer, 'a 50-year-old brunette with a healthy appetite, massive torso and solid hips. Brusque and energetic, her voice was roughened by cocktails.' The guests emptied their glasses so rapidly that the servants had difficulty collecting up the empty wine

Sebah. *An Oriental charmer.* c.1880. Postcard. Private collection

bottles which the guests deposited under the table, leaving them to go rolling around on the floor under their feet.

The entertainment began with a singer from the Opéra. She was in the middle of a song when the hostess emerged from her drunken stupor:

'Enough Debussy! Hallo! Give us the Persian! We want the Persian!'

The singer turned white. The sheet music trembled in her little clenched hands. She smiled like a child who is just about to burst into tears.

'Pardon, Madame. You will not be seeing the Persian this evening,' I said, just as indignant on behalf of the singer as for those of us to whom this dead-drunk Herodias had barked out her orders.

'What's that?' she asked, her wine-fuddled eyes opening wide.

'Our art is far too sad for such a happy crowd.' I turned my back on her, as did my Hindu musicians. After some inarticulate spluttering she began hurling ornaments onto the floor. Even the table went rolling, in her hysterical outburst.

My friend the Russian diplomat came up to me, also a little drunk. 'Always dramas!' he laughed, knowing very well my mania for taking everything in deadly earnest.

'Why did you bring me here to this Messalina of the Markets?' I said indignantly.

'You're wrong. She's a good sort, the best sort I know,' he assured me, a little confused.[60]

Armen was taken up by the artists and intellectuals of the city, and in this cosmopolitan crowd she breathed more freely than in the salons of the wealthy. Yet neither audience really pleased her. Becoming increasingly distanced from her public persona, and describing herself now in the third person, she admitted that she had come to hate the necessary commercialism of her art, offered up to an audience for whom she had little respect. And though she continued to accept engagements in order to pay her bills, she lost all love of the dance and turned to writing instead.

Dancer from Tripoli. 1920s. Postcard.
Private collection

Contemporary reviews indicate that, in the eyes of a European audience, she conformed to the mould of 'acceptable' dance. Delicate and ethereal, she seems to have satisfied her audience's expectation of Oriental dance, which was worlds away from the earthy abandon and vigorous hips of Little Egypt. Armen Ohanian was fortunate in being in the right place at the right time, and being able to benefit from the flourishing Orientalism of the period. As for the other dancers from the East, in time they too adopted Western ideas, with the result that, little by little, their costume and dance underwent great changes.

Passing through Egypt on her way to Europe in the early years of the present century, Armen Ohanian lamented the start of Western influence on the dance:

> In Cairo one evening I saw, with sick, incredulous eyes, one of our most sacred dances degraded into a horrible bestiality. It

115

was our poem of the mystery and pain of motherhood. In olden Asia, which has kept the dance in its early purity, it represents maternity, the mysterious conception of life, the suffering and joy with which a new soul is brought into the world... But the spirit of the West had touched this holy dance and it had become the *hoochie koochie*, the *danse du ventre*, the belly dance. I heard the lean Europeans chuckling, I even saw lascivious smiles upon the lips of Asiatics, and I fled.[61]

Chapter 6

THE OBSESSIVE IMAGE

Those were the years when artists felt the need to be reborn. In order to be reborn, they had to find their way back to nature again, to the primitive, and, above all, to the self.

Walter Sorell, *Dance in its Time*

Throughout the first two decades of the twentieth century dance was the most influential of the arts in the West. It was during this period that European and American dance was transformed from being a mere diversion into an art capable of expressing the most profound experiences of life. This metamorphosis was brought about by a handful of pioneering individuals whose inspiration largely derived from ancient Greece and the Middle East. The contemporary attitude to dance at the turn of the century can be summed up by a music critic who wrote about Isadora Duncan — the genius behind the reshaping and expansion of theatrical dance — that, until she appeared, dance had no validity other than as a diversion. No intellectual gave the dance serious consideration; either it appeared as a mere social activity or it took the form of ballet, a favourite diversion of 'old gentlemen known as balletomanes'.

Isadora Duncan was the first to challenge current assumptions with her claim that dance was not only an expression of human beauty, but could be as profoundly moving as great drama and poetry. In her early career she was inspired above all by her understanding of ancient Greek dance, though she later came to realize that it was the spirit rather than the form of ancient Greece which had originally motivated her; her dance was essentially her own invention.

By far the greatest source of inspiration for new dance was the Orient. And although no distinction was made between the dance of the Middle and Far East, not to speak of North Africa, most Oriental dancers were unconsciously struggling to imitate Egyptian *baladi*, though their own individual styles

Colinet Clair. *Dancer from Thebes, on a base depicting scenes from Pharaonic frescos.* 1930s. Bronze and ivory figure. Private collection

Descamps. *The Charleston.* 1930s. Bronze and ivory figure. Private collection

bore little resemblance to the original. Orientalism had been percolating down through public awareness for a number of years. Many a middle-class Western home had its Arab corner, complete with potted palms and Persian rugs; the fashion for Turkish harem trousers had been and gone; various artists had experimented with hashish, finding in it a more expansive source of inspiration that the 'ignoble, heavy drunkenness' of alcohol, as Théophile Gautier put it.

Yet while members of the public proved eager to embrace Oriental dance, they insisted that it conform to their own fantasies. Consequently, a refined, Westernized Oriental dance took shape, a combination of upper torso movement, dramatic poses and ritual mime. Explicit movements of the hips were taboo for those who performed in 'artistic' circles. Between them, the legion of amateurs and professionals fashioned an Oriental dance capable of accommodating everyone's fantasies of the East without offending too many people. Colette performed such a dance in café concerts and at society parties, and has left us with some delicately etched studies based on her experience there.

Colette grew up in an age which saw a metamorphosis in women's role in society. Within her lifetime, women were to emerge from their decorative chrysalis to become the active, short-skirted career girls and flappers of the twenties. During this period fashion altered dramatically. The constricting outfits which hampered the free movement of the body and were the cause of illness and deformity gave way to a graceful, flowing costume which was inspired by the new dance.

Fashion, the arts and social lifestyle are interdependent. Developments in one of these fields are rarely isolated, but are inspired by and, in turn, nourish the others. One of the changes during this period concerned the status of public performers. Colette, who turned to music hall in order to gain financial independence after divorcing her first husband, was keenly aware that, in the eyes of the world, she had lost all dignity when she joined 'the profession of those without a profession', as she called it. In 1906, in a letter to a friend thanking him for sending her a parcel of books, she wrote (we may suspect with tongue in cheek) that she intended to discontinue their correspondence because appearing on the stage humiliated her in his eyes. With customary humour she added that, as he could see, she knew very well how to keep her place.

Professional dance at that time was the province of ballet and music hall. Most young girls were driven onto the stage through poverty. They came from desperately poor homes and in time became the main breadwinners of the family. From the mid-nineteenth century onwards children were engaged to dance in pantomime, undernourished mites whose hours of work were gruelling and whose duties included fetching and carrying for adult members of the company. They spent their free time sitting with their feet in a peculiarly agonizing pair of stocks, which induced the power of pointing the toes until they formed a line with the legs. In later years, as members of the corps de ballet, it cannot have been easy to resist the financial blandishments of stage-door Johnnies, the aristocrats and self-made businessmen who idled about backstage with offers of protection.

Although ballet — a dance which derives from the court entertainment of the sixteenth century — was the delight of kings, most ballerinas were regarded as of dubious moral character. One nineteenth-century English dancer was refused the sacrament purely on the grounds of her occupation. The stage had long been linked with debauchery. All performers were tarred with the same brush, whatever their personal life. The most celebrated courtesans of the nineteenth century used the theatre as their shop window, while their less elevated sisters attracted attention by parading up and down the promenade at the back. There have always been entertainers whose artistry has enabled them to rise above the generally low status of their profession, performers who have been sought after and treated as social equals by the ruling classes of every land. For the majority, however, this was not the case.

The ballerina was engaged for her beauty and vivacity rather than her ability to dance. If she could dance, so much the better, but it was of little consequence. Her principal task was to look good and, with the gradual raising of ballet skirts during the nineteenth century, to smile and display her

Sheet music cover. 1922

Western fantasies of Oriental dance.
1900-20. Photographs. Private
collection

legs. The propriety of ballerinas' dresses was a constant topic of debate. While bosoms were openly displayed, legs were not revealed until the introduction of 'fleshings' at the Paris Opéra, after the French Revolution. The Pope subsquently decreed that, in theatres under his jurisdiction, these transparent tights must be blue, so that they did not suggest flesh and incite wantonness of thought. (Piano legs were draped in Victorian England for much the same reason.)

Legs were the focus of Western dance, and the principal object of erotic contemplation. The cult of the leg was pursued most fervently in France and reached its apotheosis in the can-can, a dance which was banned in England. In America, when a burlesque dancer attempted to dance the can-can and raised her foot twelve inches off the stage, the entire audience shouted 'Whoooooo' and the show became the talk of the town.

Aside from ballet and opera, which included short dance sequences to add variety to the programme, theatre dance was found in music halls, where performers were less skilled than the ballet girls with whom they were generally grouped indiscriminately together. The music hall or vaudeville show was a cross between satirical revue, operetta and pageant, with dance turns which parodied the ballet.

In America ballet was known only through occasional visits by European touring companies. There, theatre dance consisted of the jigs, reels, skirt dances and high kicks of vaudeville, dances which had arrived with immigrants from England and Ireland. Vaudeville's poor relation was burlesque, which came out of the honky tonks and other low dives in which men dressed as women acted as decoys to attract customers. (Having women do this work was too fraught with peril even to be considered.) One burlesque artist of the time recalls that there were women then who would not walk down the side of the street that contained a burlesque theatre.

Following the 1893 Great Columbia Exposition and the introduction of Little Egypt, the *hoochie koochie* became a feature of American burlesque. It was advertised as the highlight of the show and was placed at the top of the bill, just before the curtain came down. One of these *hooch* dancers was the 'unspeakably frank' Millie de Leon:

> From knee to neck she was convulsive. Every muscle became eloquent of primitive emotion. Standing suddenly erect, with a deft movement she revealed her nude right leg from knee almost to waist. A strut to the right, a long stride back, and the 'abdominal' dance was resumed… Streaked and sweaty, her face took on the aspect of epilepsy. She bit her lips, rolled her eyes, pulled fiercely at great handfuls of her black, curly hair. Indescribable noises and loud suggestions mingled in the hot breath of the audience. Men in the audience rose with shouts. A woman — one of six present — hissed. Laughter became uproarious. And then Millie de Leon gave a little cry that was more a yelp, and ceased.[62]

Vaudeville dancers of the time were often called Millie, not because that was their name, but because burlesque audiences were unfamiliar with French and took the abbreviation of 'Mademoiselle' for a Christian name. Fatima was another popular name, along with Kishka, Poupik and other English translations of Jewish words for the navel and other parts of the body.

The *hoochie koochie* became a byword for the ultimate in shameless dancing. In 1893 burlesque artiste Rose Sydell's shoulder strap broke in the middle of a number and she was brought before the magistrate, with a representative of the Watch and Ward Society giving evidence against her. So synonymous was the *hoochie koochie* with sinfulness that the prosecution tried to suggest Rose Sydell was performing this dance when her shoulder strap broke, although in fact she was not a *kooch* dancer at all. The judge asked for specific details of her act:

> 'Well, she wiggled her abdomen.'
> 'Just what do you mean by that?'
> 'She moved her abdomen in different ways.'
> 'Will you kindly show us?'
> 'Well, first she did this, and then she did that,' and seeming to forget his surroundings, the old man got up and began to wiggle, squirm and

Turkish cigarette packet. c.1910. *Arabesque* collection, New York

go through all sorts of contortions. Everybody in the courtroom began to roar.[63]

The case was dismissed.

Little Egypt's influence extended into the 1920s when, following the ravages of the First World War, dance became the most popular social activity. People danced as if possessed, celebrating a return to normality after a war unlike any other. Two of the most popular dance crazes of the twenties were the Charleston and the shimmy. The Charleston stylized the movements in the film of *Fatima's Dance*: a jump to one side, shaking the bottom, then a jump to the other. It was considered the limit in suggestive movement until it was eclipsed by the shimmy, another dance inspired by Little Egypt and her contemporaries, based on a vigorous shaking of the shoulders. Charleston and shimmy dresses were covered in long fringes, which served even further to emphasize the shaking of the body.

Apart from vaudeville and burlesque, American dance at the turn of the century took the form of the spectacle extravaganza. This was a lavish concoction of opera, musical, pantomime and dazzling stage effects. In 1892 a 13-year-old American girl went to see one of these extravaganzas in a New Jersey amusement park. Her name was Ruth Denis (later, as an actress in a small touring theatre company, she was to insert a 'Saint' between her first and last names). The extravaganza which she witnessed as a young girl, entitled 'Egypt through the Centuries', compressed thousands of years of Egyptian history into a pantomime display lit with new-fangled electricity. It was a melange of fact and fancy, boasting 'Eaters of serpents, Almees, Gavazies, gypsies and jugglers', as well as a 'Grand Oriental Ballet' which took the form of lines of young girls in ballet pumps parading up and down in formation.

Ruth St Denis was enthralled by this attempt at the recreation of an antique land and stored it up in her memory for future reference. Years later it surfaced when she was earning her living as an actress. She was sitting in a drugstore with friends when her eye was caught by a poster advertising Egyptian Deity cigarettes. The poster showed a bare-breasted goddess seated between the portals

Facing page:
Images of dancers, after Orientalist paintings (one after Leopold Carl Müller's *Ghaziya*, see ch.3). 1910. Postcards. Private collection

Ruth St Denis in 'The Cobra'. c.1906.
Photograph

of a temple, hands on her knees, eyes closed in a meditative pose. The position was that of a pharaonic mummy, but the face and body were those of a wholesome young American woman. St Denis recalls being hypnotized by this image and its suggestions of mystery, regal womanliness and hidden power, to the extent that she had to be dragged away by her friends. Thoughts of antiquity and of the spirituality of ancient civilizations stirred in her mind. She decided that her metier was not, after all, to be a bit player in someone else's company, but to be independent; she now determined to be primarily a dancer rather than an actress.

St Denis was essentially self-taught, like the other soloists who created what became known as interpretative dance. It was a form which flourished initially in Europe, yet was created largely by a small group of uniquely inspired Americans. Young women of genteel but impoverished backgrounds, they shared a boldness of approach, an independence that was lacking in their European contemporaries and that owed much to the American pioneering spirit and refusal to accept defeat.

Like Isadora Duncan before her, St Denis was immersed in her vision of a new dance, and was not willing to accept the taint of her profession. The dance she had in mind was not for the vaudeville stage (though she did, in her early career, present it there) but for the art world. Her main inspiration was the East, or her own particular vision of it. She based her work on the lavish performance spectacles of the time, expressing her ideas through a similar use of tableaux. Yet 'Egypta', inspired by the cigarette poster, would have cost so much to mount that she had to wait until 1910, when 'exotic' dance was sufficiently popular with the public for someone to invest the necessary money. 'Egypta' consisted of five tableaux — Invocation to the Nile, The Palace Dance, The Veil of Isis, The Dance of Day and The Hall of Judgement — each with a cast of courtiers, slave girls, soldiers and other extras, all trained by St Denis. She appeared as the central figure of each scene, clad in a semi-transparent pleated tunic and a wig braided with shells and beads, her eyes heavily outlined in the style of pharaonic frescos.

St Denis followed the tradition of theatre as

spectacle, while at the same time breaking with it. Dance had hitherto not been considered capable of carrying depth and meaning; it was merely entertainment, an interlude in opera, a light-hearted break to gladden the eye by the exhibition of female beauty. St Denis's dance emphasized the spiritual dimension of human experience, with the celebration of pagan religions via ritual ceremonies and the exploration of the concept of female deity appearing as frequent themes in her work. It was her genuine ambition to interpret the civilizations of the East for an American audience to whom such civilizations were as remote as the kingdoms of a fairy tale. In her early career, the nearest she came to seeing genuine Eastern dance was a troupe of Hindu entertainers on Coney Island. Yet for her, that was enough. Her approach is summed up in her autobiography: 'Any technique is sufficient which adequately expresses and reveals the thought intended by the artist.' She read up on her subject and relentlessly questioned all her Eastern friends and acquaintances on every aspect of their culture. Thus, little by little, her style took shape.

She took her own body as the starting-point, moulding a form around a highly personal sense of movement, just as Isadora Duncan had done. Also like Duncan, St Denis herself, rather than the dance, was the central focus of the performance, although she filled the stage with scenery and a company of other players. Her earliest work, the Indian-inspired Radha, took the form of a cycle of dances, 'The Delirium of the Senses'. This celebration of the body was something new in Western dance at the time, as was her costume: fleshings covered in costume jewellery. The Radha cycle of dances invoked each of the senses in turn. She kissed her fingertips, inhaled the fragrance of flowers and pressed them to her breast; she donned a set of finger cymbals and played them, inclining her head the better to appreciate their music; and, wrapping a golden skirt around her, with her supple spine bending slowly backwards, launched into a whirl of spinning movement which culminated in a climactic faint to the floor.

In her memoirs she records that her rippling arm movement was the subject of frequent speculation:

An Oriental beauty (after a painting by C.V. Muttich). 1915. Postcard. Private collection

Ruth St Denis and Ted Shawn. c.1916. Photograph. BBC Hulton Picture Library, London

*American dancer La Meri performing
a dance of the Maghreb.* c.1930.
Photograph. *Arabesque* collection,
New York

*Agnes De Mille as an Ouled Nail
dancer.* 1920s. Photograph.
Arabesque collection, New York

My arms were held out from the shoulder and were raised and lowered with a subtle rippling movement which began between the shoulder blades and seemed to extend through and beyond the fingers. In 'The Cobra' the arms took on the undulating ripples of the snake's body. After my Cobra dance we would frequently see women furtively practising the sinuosities of the snake dance in the orchestra stalls or at the back of their boxes.[64]

Performing in Germany one night, she was visited in her dressing room by four professors of anatomy, anxious to see this famous ripple at close quarters. Much amused, St Denis obligingly lowered her shawl over her shoulders. As she moved her arms the professors proceeded to tap them from shoulder to wrist:

> They all talked at once, and they all exclaimed in various tones, '*Das ist wunderbar*! She has no bones. Yet it doesn't stop. It goes on and on.' Finally, after more tappings, more close examinations, they clicked their heels together and bowed themselves out with many protestations of amazement and incredulity.[65]

A child of her time, St Denis created her dance and her own personal myth as she went along. Like other American dance pioneers, she was only recognized in her own country after she had been acclaimed in Europe. Even though she did not enjoy performing in vaudeville, she worked there in her early days, sandwiched between performing monkeys and fire-eaters, before she was sufficiently successful to be able to create a more suitable stage for her work.

She is interesting largely because it is through her that European and American audiences gained their first idea of Oriental dance. She went on to found the Denishawn School in California, where the actresses of Hollywood's silent screen went to learn the rudiments of dance. In those early films of the twenties and thirties, with their Biblical heroines and choruses of Babylonian dancing girls, we find the reflection of Ruth St Denis and her ideas.

No artist works in a vacuum. Sensitivity to

contemporary currents of thought is a decisive factor in inspiring a new movement in the arts. And at the turn of the century social currents were flowing powerfully in all directions. Advances in technology and the spread of industrialization were creating wealth in America and Europe, and the new middle class was able to afford an increasing range of novel consumer goods. The growth of railways and the invention of the telegraph and the motor car were helping to overcome problems of long-distance communication. The introduction of the electric light bulb in 1879 meant that it was no longer necessary to be bound by the natural rhythms of night and day. Meanwhile, on another front, Sigmund Freud was beginning to illuminate the darker recesses of the human psyche.

For a long time the arts showed little reflection of the changes taking place with such unprecedented speed. In place of a new style the public was offered revivals of earlier movements, which looked back to a golden past. This changed with the emergence of art nouveau in the 1880s. Art nouveau was a movement of its time, the first style which did not sink its roots in European history, but borrowed largely from Oriental art. Japan is often mentioned in this connection, yet art nouveau craftsmen were influenced to an equal extent by the Islamic tradition. In the late nineteenth century — just as in the sixteenth — Islamic art became a major influence on European decorative style. In form and interior design, the 'palaces' built to house the great exhibitions bore the indirect influence of Islamic art, which many designers praised for its unity and adaptability, the way in which it both stimulated the imagination and soothed the eye.

Owen Jones, who was influenced by the delicate primary colouring of the Alhambra in his interior design for London's Crystal Palace, commented on the enduring quality of Islamic design, compared to the constant search for novelty, regardless of suitability, in European art. John Frederick Lewis, who lived in Cairo in the 1840s, spent the next twenty-five years back in England recreating scenes of Egyptian life in his paintings. He too was inspired by the 'gossamer, perforated fabric' of Islamic architecture, which threw into relief the play of light on solids, lending them a shimmering, insubstantial

Erté. *Slave girl, 'Legendary Kings'.* 1919. Costume design. Private collection

Erté. *Oriental dance costume for the Folies Bergères.* 1920. Costume design. Private collection

air. In a book on Oriental carpets published in 1882, Vincent Robinson commented that the more 'elementary' lifestyle of the Middle East, where there were no art schools or institutes of higher learning, seemed to work in favour of the imagination, to judge from the work of Oriental carpet makers.

Rhythmic, flowing line, a principal feature of Islamic design, became the trademark of the art nouveau movement, which rejected the straight line in favour of a sinuous, extended curve. It sought inspiration primarily in the plant world, taking the tendrils of vegetation as a starting-point to create exaggerated, stylized swirls of movement. It took sustenance, too, from the long hair and curves of a woman's body, and subsequently showed a preoccupation with the feminine ideal which, visually speaking, was then in a process of upheaval.

The mid-Victorian woman was a heavily upholstered creature, yet also a provocative one, with the swinging hoops of her crinoline allowing glimpses of her long white underwear to appear when she moved. Turn-of-the-century fashion, while giving women a more graceful outline, was a somewhat sinister form of armour-plating. Portraits of the period often show women in profile, the better to display the ideal female form. Tilting backwards from the shoulders, her bottom thrust out, we see a woman whose serpentine body harmonizes perfectly with those exaggerated art nouveau curves. Yet while her trailing skirt may have looked elegant, it picked up mud and germs in abundance. Her wasp waist — sometimes an incredible thirteen inches — was achieved by means of corsets which all but cut the body in two. Colette tells us of an actress who refused to take any sitting parts in the theatre and was compelled to stay on her feet all evening, even during the intervals, on account of stays which made it impossible to bend her legs. Her corset was fitted with iron straps down the back and thighs, held in place between the legs; they started under the armpit and finished just above the knee.[66] Not surprisingly, these corsets did untold harm to the body, deforming the ribs, displacing and atrophying the internal organs and threatening to cut the liver in two. They were designed for 3-year-olds upwards. One American doctor who examined a class of schoolgirls, two-thirds of whom wore corsets, discovered that none was able to lift her arms above her head.

Rumblings of revolt against this fashion had been felt from the middle of the nineteenth century onwards, when various attempts were made to design a more practical 'hygienic' dress. One early experiment, 'bloomers' (invented by New York post-mistress Amelia Bloomer), were fashioned after an Oriental operetta costume and consisted of a bodice and knee-length skirt above voluminous Turkish pantaloons. In 1898 a 'new reform dress' made its appearance in Germany. It had a high neck, no waistline and long full sleeves gathered at the wrist. This outfit, worn at a dress reform convention at which dance had been arranged to demonstrate how much more easily the body could move in such a garment, did not catch the imagination for, although practical, it was neither flattering nor elegant.

In 1906 Paul Poiret designed a gown to be worn with a new kind of rubberized corset. This style of costume, the end product of many years of searching for an acceptable reform dress, took its inspiration from ancient Greece via Isadora Duncan. Poiret was an admirer of Duncan's work. Like her, he realized that the natural point of support in the body was provided by the shoulders, not the waist. His gowns not only flattered the body, they made it look supremely graceful, as well as allowing a woman to breathe freely. It only took a few years for other couturiers to follow Poiret in designing gowns which were gathered under the breast and draped down the back in a classical, flowing line. Fashion writers began describing their new creations in terms of dance, the art which lay behind the emerging twentieth-century woman.

Released from its rigid whalebone scaffolding, the torso was set free for the serpentine movements of Oriental dance, with its supple, undulating spine. There were various reasons for its growing popularity. For one thing, it was essentially self-expressive. It appealed to an age in which the arts were tending increasingly towards subjectivity and the evocation of mood and emotion. Not only was it a solo art which did not require a partner, it had connotations of mystery and hidden sensuality which appealed to women as much as to men.

Paul Poiret. *Design for a Persian ballet.* Poster

Facing page, top:
Raoul Larche. *The Veil Dance, inspired by Lois Fuller.* c.1890. Art nouveau figure. Private collection

---

Facing page, bottom:
George Woodall. *Serpentina.* c.1895. Wheel-carved cameo vase. Private collection

Facing page:
Colette. 1910. Photograph. Roger
Viollet collection, Paris

Barrias. *Young girl from Bou Saada.*
c.1900. Gilt bronze figure. Private
collection

One way of indicating this mysterious allure was the use of the veil, that ubiquitous symbol of the Eastern female. Beloved of the art nouveau artist, veils were an important item of costume for the army of exotic interpreters who began appearing at smart parties and on the public stage. Society hostesses were among the many who pieced together an Oriental act consisting of theatrical poses, 'passionate writhings', angular mock pharaonic gestures and the discarding of veils in a graceful manner.

Gertrude Vanderbilt Whitney took lessons from Ruth St Denis, and was one of the best known (as well as being among the first) American women to perform an Oriental dance. It was quite the thing at society parties, even for the hostess, to give an impromptu performance, although, more often than not, professional performers and musicians were hired to entertain at these Oriental soirées. In 1911 Poiret gave an Arabian ball, a grand affair at which he greeted his guests with Persian songs and invited those among them not suitably dressed to select a costume for the night from his collection of Persian clothes. Meanwhile actor Edouard de Max read aloud in the main salon from the *One Thousand and One Nights*.

In her novel *La Vagabonde*, Colette draws on her own experience as a professional dancer to describe a society party she attended:

> My hand trembling with stage fright, I wrap myself in the veil which constitutes almost my entire costume, a circular veil of blue and violet, measuring fifteen yards round. I begin to writhe as my hands slowly loosen. Little by little the veil unwinds, fills, billows out and falls, revealing me to the eyes of the audience, who have stopped their frantic chatter to gaze at me... I dance and dance. A beautiful serpent coils itself along the Persian carpet, an Egyptian amphora tilts forward, pouring forth a cascade of perfumed hair, a blue and stormy cloud rises and floats away, a feline beast springs forwards, then recoils; a sphinx, the colour of pale sand, reclines at full length, propped on its elbows with hollowed back and straining breasts.[67]

Colette gained a certain notoriety for appearing bare-breasted in a music hall revue. She was rare in revealing her body, for most dancers to appear in the nude generally wore fleshings. These fleshings covered them from neck to ankle and were adorned with various pieces of cloth and jewellery. As Colette quotes one music hall artist:

A dancer in the nude always means something in the Egyptian style, and that entails a good ten pounds' weight of beaten metal straps and belts and ornaments, beaded latticework on the legs, necklaces from here to there and no end of veils.[68]

Performing in decorated fleshings was considered greatly daring in those days when, it should be remembered, the sight of Isadora Duncan's bare legs and feet was enough to cause a public scandal.

What was Colette like as a dancer? One critic thought her the most original of the mimes, the most spontaneous and disturbing. Another was of a different opinion and found her heavy-footed and lacking all sense of choreographic drama. His review ends with the comment:

There was much ignorance and presumption concerning the art of the dance, which after all is a little more difficult than playing with a skipping rope. But this was the moment of juvenile and inconsequent performances.[69]

A number of dancers claimed Oriental descent in order to give themselves an air of greater credibility. One of these was Mata Hari, who enjoyed considerable critical success as an Oriental dancer and was known in her heyday as *la femme la plus célèbre d'Europe*. Colette, who had a sharp eye (and an even sharper pen) when it came to the absurdities of the Oriental dance craze, dispensed with Mata Hari's act in a few words. Yet one review spoke of her as the superior even of Duncan:

Words may give an idea of the beauty and poetry of [her] dances, but nothing inanimate will render the emotion conveyed by the performer, nor the colour or harmony of the Eastern figure.

Edmund Dulac. *Morgiana, heroine of
'Ali Baba and the 40 Thieves', from the
'Tales of 1001 Nights'.* Book
illustration

It was a tropical plant in all its richness,
transplanted to a Northern soil.[70]

Mata Hari claimed descent from a temple dancer
of the Far East. In order further to confound her
critics, she introduced her act as 'sacred' dance
learned in the very precincts of her mother's temple.
In 1905, when she was enjoying her first tentative
success in Paris, she met Emile Guimet, a leading
Orientalist of the time. He was knowledgeable
enough to realize that she was an imposter in every
way; yet his business instincts prompted him to
gamble on a woman who was already making a name
for herself in high society. He offered her the pick
of his collection of Oriental silks and jewellery, to
be worn at a performance which he was prepared
to sponsor in his museum of antiquities.

No detail of the performance was overlooked,
even down to creating intimate lighting by concealing
red candles behind glass panels all around the
performance area. Into an atmosphere heavy with
incense stepped Mata Hari, treading lightly on the
rose petals strewn over the floor. Her performance
was a triumph and she found herself inundated with
requests to appear at private parties.

She was now successfully launched on her career,
and had she been more circumspect and a better
judge of the changing times, she might have avoided
the tragedy of her later life. But sound judgement
was not one of her qualities. Dance was initially a
means to an end, a way of earning a living in the
manner of other courtesans by parading her charms
before prospective protectors. Now, however,
carried away by her audience's enthusiasm as well
as the ecstatic reviews she was receiving, she began
to think of herself as a serious artist. In her attempts
to secure engagements in the more respected world
of opera and serious theatre, she was to meet failure
time and time again.

She became obsessed by the idea of appearing in
Diaghilev's Ballets Russes, which was then at the
height of its creative and popular success. The
Ballets Russes had replaced the whimsical
Orientalism of art nouveau with a savage and richly
colourful East. Diaghilev's aim was total theatre, a
synthesis of music, drama and movement. Although
he could have taken any one of these as the main

vehicle for his ideas, it was dance that he chose. Dance was then the most articulate of all the arts, the centre of a shifting kaleidoscope of creative invention. Bakst's multi-layered, multi-coloured costumes for Diaghilev's 1910 production of 'Sheherazade', with their semi-transparent chiffons, contributed to the public outrage with which the ballet was greeted.

The scandalous reputation of the Ballets Russes derived mainly from its modernity and its frank attitude to subjects that were still taboo, rather than the occasional sight of nude flesh. Perhaps Mata Hari believed her daring reputation gave her something in common with Diaghilev's company and that, for this reason alone, she had something to offer them. As it happened, they shared the same agent in Gabriel Astruc, who was frankly surprised when Mata Hari announced her desire to work with the company. At first Diaghilev brushed off Astruc's suggestion that he audition her. In the end he agreed, principally as a favour to Astruc, though he had no intention of engaging her. Having better things to do with his time than audition a dancer he did not want, he turned the matter over to Bakst who, it seems, enjoyed himself at Mata Hari's expense by asking her to undress rather than dance. Only after he had taken a good look at the famous body did he tell her there was no opening for her with the company.

It was one of a long series of humiliations. Mata Hari failed to realize that she no longer had her old drawing power. Her initial success had given rise to a host of imitators, and Oriental dancers were now two a penny, younger, fresher talents with more daring ideas than hers. Mata Hari, who relied on her beauty and the novelty of her act to attract attention, needed to keep one step ahead of her rivals, and this she failed to do. The notion that she could ever have fitted in with Diaghilev's company was only one of her many errors of judgement, which were eventually to lead to her arrest and conviction on charges of spying.

She could be excused for imagining the Ballets Russes might be a vehicle for her talents, for they were, after all, exploring the Oriental theme. Sheherazade, Cleopatra and Salome were all the subject of ballets during this period — a series of

Leon Bakst. *Bacchanale*. c.1900. Costume design for the Ballets Russes. Private collection

Aimé Stevens. *Anna Pavlova in a Syrian dance*. 1920. Pastel. Private collection

135

dark and powerful heroines that were a far cry from Mata Hari's supposed sacred dancer of the East.

We cannot go back in time and see the vaudeville artists, society dancers and ballet girls of the period. Nevertheless their influence is felt in early Hollywood movies, one of whose favourite characters was the Biblical heroine, the enchantress of the East. Stories from the Bible gave ample opportunity for diversion in the shape of troupes of dancing girls. Cecil B. De Mille frequently included flashbacks to the ancient world, even when his films were set in the present day. These flashbacks, ostensibly used to compare the manners of two contrasting periods, provided the excuse for scenes of orgiastic revelry, complete with dancing girls.

In the days before the advent of sound, film required a different style of acting than the grand

Dancing girls of Babylon, from 'Intolerance' by D.W. Griffith. 1916. Film still. Museum of Modern Art, New York

gestures of nineteenth-century theatre, in which a story unfolded through language. Directors soon came to understand the necessity of creating a new language for the movies — one based on the vocabulary of the body. In the early days of film, gesture, facial expression, repose and rhythmic movement were the key to revealing character; thus a dance background was thought to be a more useful qualification for Hollywood than theatrical experience.

Directors explored the power of dance to hold an audience's attention without the necessity of words, as well as to evoke a sensual mood. Most of D.W. Griffith's actresses had originally been dancers. He had a keen understanding of the inherent possibilities in dance, which he used as a metaphor for climactic moments in his work. In a well-known scene from *Intolerance*, the camera pans down the steps of Babylon where scores of dancers (trained by Ruth St Denis) celebrate the city's victory in movements which conjure up the frescos of pharaonic Egypt. Close-ups on the steps of the Temple of Ishtar show the amatory rites of 'sacred prostitutes', glimpsed through a haze of incense smoke and fountain spray.

It is ironic that while a surprising degree of nudity was accepted in early Hollywood movies, and though one of their most frequent features was the Western fantasy of Arabic dance, one of the first films to be censored was the innocuous *Fatima's Dance*, as we have seen. The public's taste in heroines may have shifted from the pure Victorian heroine to the *femme fatale*, but most Hollywood *femmes fatales* were wholesome, nubile young girls with rosebud lips. When they danced, even though their costumes may have been diaphanous, they did not do anything as unacceptable as thrust their pelvises.

Film vamp Theda Bara, whose name is an anagram of 'Arab death', was a different kind of *femme fatale*, a woman with a darkly brooding look and heavily kohl-rimmed eyes. She was an early example of a star whose personality was manufactured by the studio publicity department. Stories about her stressed the strange and macabre. It was told that she was born in the shadow of the pyramids and weaned on serpents' blood; that her father was a desert shaikh; that a lover had committed suicide in her dressing room. She wore Middle Eastern dress,

Untitled film still from the turn of the century. Arabesque collection, New York

Theda Bara in 'Salome'. 1918. Film still. Museum of Modern Art, New York

Facing page:
John Reinhard Weguelin. *Herodias and her daughter.* Late 19th century. Oil painting. Private collection

pretended not to speak English and had a Nubian footman who drove her around in her white limousine.

The vamp's costume was the forerunner of today's cabaret dress: ornamented breastplates and a skirt resting on the hips, revealing the legs through its transparent folds. In the kind of heavy symbolism beloved of film in its early days, the serpent theme was used in every possible way; we even find it in a particularly uncomfortable-looking pair of metallic breastplates shaped like two coiled snakes, which were made for Theda Bara.

The film vamp was based on the stereotype of the Oriental woman and was in vogue from the turn of the century. Yet this image of the all-devouring woman proved too heartless for women to identify with and in time gave way to the *femme fatale*, who inflicted suffering on herself as well as on others. She found her most persistent expression in the figure of Salome, the archetypal dancing temptress.

One of the most intriguing manifestations of the Oriental dance craze was the Salome mania of 1907-09. During this two-year period a succession of Salomes, complete with papier mâché heads on plates, appeared in opera and popular theatre. Until that time Salome had made little impression on Western art. An obscure Biblical figure who is dispensed with in the space of a few lines without ever being mentioned by name, we find few representations of her in the arts before the late nineteenth century.

To the mediaeval mind dance was the devil's business and the devil's daughter was Salome. We find her on the porch of Rouen Cathedral balancing on her hands like a mediaeval mountebank, indeed, she is always shown performing after the custom of the day. Thus in the early nineteenth century Gustave Moreau portrayed her in 'The Apparition' gliding forward on her toes like a ballerina. She only surfaced from relative obscurity at the turn of the century, when women were beginning to express a public enjoyment of the body through a dance known for its erotic nature.

As we have seen (ch.1), Salome's dance was originally part of an allegory on the death and rebirth of nature, expressing an ancient belief in women's magical powers of fertility. The Biblical reworking

of this myth reverses its original meaning, making Salome a symbol of the dark, destructive power of women.

Oscar Wilde was the first to explore this theme in the nineteenth century with his play *Salome*, originally written in French. Refused a licence in London on the grounds that it was illegal to portray Biblical characters on the English stage, Wilde's play was first mounted in Paris in 1896. His early ideas for the work are far more interesting than his final version. Among his rejected scenarios is a chaste Salome who dances for Herod out of divine inspiration in order to protect her religion. In her eyes the Baptist is an imposter, a false prophet who threatens the Jewish God whom she worships.

Wilde used the title 'The Decapitation of Salome' for an early draft of the play. In this version Salome is banished by Herod and goes out into the desert where she lives for years, scorned and alone, dressing in animal skins and living on locusts and wild honey, as the Baptist had done. One day, when crossing a frozen lake, she falls through the ice and is decapitated. On the surface of the re-formed ice passers-by see her severed head, like the stamen of a flower surrounded by rubies. Unfortunately, this wonderful art nouveau image, coupled with an interesting variant on the religious theme of the tale, was not the one which Wilde eventually chose. In his final version Salome takes revenge on the Baptist out of frustrated passion for him.

Wilde was a great admirer of Huysmans' novel *A Rebours* (1884), the bible of the Decadent movement, to which Wilde subscribed. Huysmans' hero, the world-weary Des Esseintes, lives the life of a recluse. He surrounds himself with exotica, chosen to stimulate the senses, among which we find Moreau's two portraits of Salome. Des Esseintes ponders at length on the significance of the story. For him, Salome has always remained elusive:

> lost in a mysterious ecstasy far off in the mists of time, beyond the reach of punctilious, pedestrian minds, [eluded by all artists, who have] never succeeded in rendering the disquieting delirium of the dancer, the subtle grandeur of the murderess.[71]

Facing page:
Gustave Moreau. *The Apparition*. Oil painting. Gustave Moreau Museum, Paris

In Moreau's portraits, Des Esseintes finds the superhuman figure of his dreams. Obsessed with unravelling the deeper meaning of the story, he examines every detail of the paintings. Looking at the sacred lotus blossom which Salome holds between her breasts, he asks, does this flower suggest the sacrifice of virginity, or does it represent the allegory of fertility? Or — and this is the explanation he appears to prefer, for he dwells on it at length — is Salome 'the symbolic incarnation of undying lust, the Goddess of immortal Hysteria... a true harlot, obedient to her passionate and cruel female temperament'?

Huysmans rejects the connection with fertility, just as Wilde abandoned a scenario in which Salome acts in defence of her religion. It is tempting to ask whether the Salome craze would otherwise have taken the form it did. As it was, Salome became the archetypal dancing seductress, and those who came after Wilde followed his scenario, even down to having her kiss the Baptist's severed head as it lay dripping on its silver charger. In Strauss's opera, performed at the New York Metropolitan Opera in 1907, the way in which Salome fondled the severed head so 'sickened the public stomach' that the production had to be withdrawn after only one night.

From opera Salome moved into vaudeville and the sophisticated New York Ziegfeld Follies. Gertrude Hoffman, a talented comic vaudeville dancer, was dispatched to London to draw some inspiration from Maud Allan, who played at the Palace Theatre for months, with queues stretching all around the block to see her. (Ironically, Isadora Duncan was performing to sparse audiences only a few streets away.) Hoffman returned to New York to give the first non-comic performance of her career.

Even Ruth St Denis toyed with the idea of playing Salome. The decadent representations of the others, however, held no appeal for St Denis, who intended to remain faithful to the Bible story. The German poet-philosopher Hugo von Hoffmannsthal worked on a scenario with her which might have been the most interesting Salome of all, but it came to nothing. Hoffmannsthal believed that poetic experience could not be fully expressed in theatrical terms through speech alone; at certain climactic moments in life, dramatic bodily movement was the sole means of conveying powerful experience. He left notes outlining his ideas for Ruth St Denis's Salome:

> Every limb being tested, vain self-enjoyment of the limbs' own harmonies. Everything is here to serve, each sphere and form of nature used up by this servitude... In front of an idol under whose deadly eyes the gratified elation becomes torture. [72]

St Denis did not stay in Europe to work with Hoffmannsthal, however. Homesick for America, she went back to California and founded her school, Denishawn.

Many years later she returned to the theme of Salome, and a film was made of her rehearsing the part. She is handed seven veils in turn and plays with each of them in different ways before casually dropping them. In between are dramatic gestures and poses and little sideways movements across the stage on her toes. Though this film is a disappointing look at an influential dancer, it reinforces the descriptions which have come down to us of those other Salomes, who mixed mime with a modicum of dance and whose costumes were held together by strings of pearls. Alone of all the writers who sought to convey the essence of Salome's dance, Flaubert described the true women's dance of the Middle East. His Salome performs to flutes, finger cymbals and:

> the funereal sound of the pipes. Her poses suggested sighs, and her whole body was so languid that one could not tell whether she were mourning for a god or expiring in his embrace. With her eyes half-closed she twisted her body backwards and forwards, making her belly rise and fall and her breasts quiver, while her face remained expressionless. [73]

Last in a long line of Salomes came Mata Hari. In 1907 Strauss turned down her agent's suggestion that she take the role in his opera, choosing instead the saucy Mademoiselle Bianca Froelich. Several years later, when Mata Hari was no longer fashionable, she finally had her chance — only it was not before an adoring audience but for a private party at the home of an elderly Italian prince. Mata Hari was by now accepting every engagement which came her way. She travelled to a remote provincial town in Sicily to perform for the kind of fee she would have scorned under normal circumstances. She gave her final performance in Holland a few months after the outbreak of the First World War, for once retaining her veils. The audience was disappointed. Mata Hari blamed their conservatism for her poor reception and the war for interrupting her career.

In 1915 she set off for her beloved Paris. She was 39 now, and her hair was beginning to turn grey. But Paris had changed. With her characteristic oblivion to the outside world, Mata Hari little imagined the city would have altered in response to war. Her extravagant hats, her ostrich feathers and hobble skirts made her conspicuous in a city where attention to fashion was considered self-indulgent and out of place. The patriotic fare served up in the theatres was designed to boost the morale of the troops, and was not at all in Mata Hari's line.

Desperate for money, she accepted propositions from both the French and German governments to spy for them. In the event, she did not provide either country with a scrap of useful information. Perhaps she did not intend to. She clearly never once considered the implications of the dangerous work she had undertaken. The kind of life she lived, dependent on her beauty and charm and the patronage of wealthy admirers, had little place for attachment to any particular country. She had never made friends with women. Other courtesans were said to have disliked her; dressmakers found her difficult and demanding; even Colette, whose writing is infused with sympathy for the plight of women who relied on their bodies for their livelihood, did not have a kind word to say for her.

In 1917 Mata Hari was arrested for spying. No substantial evidence has ever been produced against her, and some writers have suggested that she provided a scapegoat for the public when attention needed to be diverted from France's failures in the war. Perhaps she was already damned for the life she had led. A woman who had risen to prominence by displaying her body in dances of an erotic nature, who had lived by selling her favours and, according

Facing page:
Reutlinger. *Mata Hari*. Photographs.
BBC Hulton Picture Library, London

to some, caused the financial ruin of more than one man, did not receive any sympathy from the public.

Mata Hari, who had played out the role of the dancing temptress in real life as well as on the stage, was condemned to death and died at the hands of the firing squad. Her body was never claimed, and was subsequently used by medical students for practising post mortems. At her trial she was described as 'this sinister Salome who plays games with the heads of French soldiers'. Ironically, her carefully fabricated myth had rebounded on her in the end.

The *femme fatale* is an archetype which has possessed the human imagination for thousands of years, and in the life of Mata Hari we find the strange excess of this obsessive image. The frequency with which Salome appears as a theme in the performing arts shows the power of the archetype in our subconscious. Yet even though films and operas of Salome sometimes aim for authenticity in their settings and costuming, the story itself still follows Wilde's version, and Salome's dance rarely resembles, even remotely, that of a woman from the Middle East.

CABARETS AND CLUBS

Chapter 7

*See the female abdomen execute such feats as never
before entered your wildest and most
unrestrained imagination.*

Julian Hawthorne

A few years ago the owner of a Cairo nightclub who
was heavily in debt asked Samia Gamal if she would
appear on a Monday evening (the traditional quiet
night) as a guest artiste. Samia Gamal is one of the
legendary dancers of the 1930s and 1940s and was
well past her dancing days, yet she agreed to give
a special performance to help him out. On the night
in question he was inundated with customers, old
and young, who wanted to see the great dancer one
more time. Her Monday nights became a regular
feature, the word spread and the club was regularly
packed out to such an extent that the owner declared
he might as well close for the rest of the week, he
did such good business on Mondays.

To the Western way of thinking, Arabic dance
has, until very recently, been more or less
synonymous with cabaret establishments. At one
end of this scale is an act which combines Arabic
dance movements, Western notions of glamour and
echoes of the Oriental dance of early Hollywood. At
the other end is the sexy turn performed by women
who know little or nothing about the dance, but who
use it as a convenient money-spinner in which the
only skill required is the ability to parade around in
a revealing costume.

Until recently there were few venues for Arabic
dance other than clubs and restaurants; hence the
finest performers of the past necessarily carved out
their careers there. Despite the restrictions of the
cabaret milieu, dancers such as Tahia Carioca and
Samia Gamal in the early days, and Nagua Fouad,
Mona Said and Asa Sharif in the 1970s and 1980s
have created their own innovations within this
context, providing a source of inspiration for today's
dancers.

The cabaret style developed in the 1920s in the nightspots of Algiers, Beirut and Cairo which sprang up, in the first instance, to satisfy the demands of a colonial audience. In her autobiography, the great Egyptian singer Umm Kulthum describes the boom in this type of establishment in Cairo after the First World War. Muhammad Ali Street in particular became notorious for its pleasure palaces and low dives. Ironically, the street was named after the nineteenth-century ruler who had banned the dancing girls from Cairo!

By the 1920s Egypt had established itself as the centre of the entertainment industry, through which it exported its ideas to the rest of the Arab world. Films were especially popular, with their rags-to-riches plots in which dancers often featured as heroines, working-class women who sought to escape their poverty through a connection with the wealthy. Cabaret dancing invariably featured in these films, even if only as a brief diversion from the main plot. Hollywood exerted the greatest influence on

Samia Gamal with Farid al-Atrache. 1930s. Film still. *Arabesque* collection, New York

film then, and its fantasy of Oriental dance filtered through and was taken up and unconsciously parodied by Arab dancers in their desire to emulate Western behaviour and modes of fashion. The first Egyptian cabaret, the Casino Opera, was opened in 1926 in Cairo by Syrian actress-dancer Badia Masabni. Badia's offered a varied bill of all-round entertainment, including an innovatory 6 o'clock matinée for women only, which was packed out every evening. With an eye on Western entertainment, she then decided to broaden the scope of Egyptian *baladi*.

Until then, the upper torso and arms had not played a particular role in *baladi*. Traditionally, the arms were simply lifted and held. Now dancers started using them to describe flowing, serpentine patterns of movement. On Masabni's extended stage, performers also began to explore the use of space, whereas they had previously performed more or less on the spot. Another of Masabni's innovations was the use of veils. The manipulation of gossamer

Samia Gamal in a cabaret costume of the 1930s. Film still. *Arabesque* collection, New York

veils was not a feature of *baladi*, it was the creation of Western Oriental dancers at the turn of the century. A reflection of how small a part it played in traditional *baladi*, today's cabaret entertainers do little with the veil except circle the stage flourishing it before casting it aside. (Western dancers have made some interesting innovations in the use of the veil, but those who create their dance around the discarding of veils would do well to consider the fact that a dancer who removes parts of her costume in this way is regarded by an Arab audience in a very dubious light.)

Two of the women who trained with Masabni, Tahia Carioca and Samia Gamal, went on to become the most celebrated dancers of their day. Samia Gamal, a slim woman in her youth, was at home with the Western fantasy element which began entering the dance in the late 1920s. It was she who broke with the custom of dancing barefoot, and it is ironic that her reason for wearing high-heeled shoes on stage was to prove that she could afford them. It was one of many innovations which led to fundamental changes in *baladi*. It was not uncommon for dancers performing out of doors to wear slippers to protect their feet from the heat. Yet high heels give a different emphasis to the dance — they change its earthy nature and low centre of gravity. The

Tahia Carioca in a baladi costume. 1930s. Film still. *Arabesque* collection, New York

same is true of the waltz-like pirouetting which became part of the new choreographed (as opposed to improvised) *baladi* pioneered by Masabni's dancers.

Extracts from old Egyptian feature films show us what *baladi* looked like at this moment of transition, when it was beginning to lose its traditional form. In those days, cabaret dancing, performed by its most respected exponents, was known as *raks al-hawanem* ('dance of the ladies'). The nuances of this style can best be seen in old clips of Tahia Carioca, who mingles reserve, decorum and an extraordinary sweetness of expression with a rather mysterious smile. It is a subtly sensuous style, while still retaining its earthiness and the heaviness of traditional *baladi*. Tahia Carioca's direct descendant among contemporary nightclub dancers is Suhair Zaki, who has not been influenced by the razzamatazz which is so much a part of the cabaret act today. Her dances are plain, her costumes relatively unadorned; she often wears a *baladi* dress which covers her from head to foot, unlike the two-piece costume which came in with other innovations during the twenties. These *baladi* dresses are especially popular in Egypt, though less so in other Arab countries. It will be recalled that dancers were

'Liz' Jamal in siren pose. 1950s. Photograph. *Arabesque* collection, New York

Following page:
Claudette Colbert in 'Cleopatra'. 1934. Film still. Museum of Modern Art, New York

formerly accustomed to perform in their everyday dress. Special costumes are the product of a highly developed theatrical tradition which did not obtain in the Arab world.

In the 1920s a costume emerged which largely owed its inspiration to Hollywood, where female allure was associated with the vamp. The Western Oriental dance outfit, a combination of bra, low-slung gauzy skirt with side slits and bare midriff, was adopted by Arab dancers and became the cabaret uniform. Dancers have never been allowed to show their navels; hence the long strip of material running vertically from the centre of a dancer's bra to join up with her skirt which we see in early films. Later on came the jewel in the navel. Today dancers overcome the injunction to cover up by sewing a flesh-coloured body stocking onto their costume bra.

This cabaret costume has altered little, in essence, since its creation in the twenties. However, such changes as there have been have merely served to rob it of its early charm, which partly derived from its suggestion of the antique. Today's bra and hip-belt encrusted with rhinestones and sequins are a more brassy version of Hollywood's fantasy of an Oriental charmer. The heavy padding of the bra top brings to mind the fifties, when the boned support and padding of bras made a woman's breasts look like bullets, a far cry from the twenties' acceptance of a more natural body line. Today's cabaret dancers show little inclination to update this costume or even adapt it to suit individual tastes or changing fashions. It is a costume which expresses notions of glamour belonging to a certain era, and is curiously dated.

The question of dress is partly one of individual taste; it is also a question of suitability. The main purpose of this type of costume is to show off the body. Bare flesh can be a great distraction, as can swinging fringes and the reflected light of thousands of rhinestones and sequins, and as the number of distractions grows we notice the dance itself less and less. Any dancer who wants to express the more complex aspects of Arabic dance cannot do so in a costume whose main purpose is to make her look like a doll.

Arab governments have repeatedly tried to suppress cabaret dancing by means of costume

regulations and by refusing to issue licences to clubs which include dance in their programme. Just as in the nineteenth century the dancers were banished from Cairo, there was a move several years ago by Muslim fundamentalists in Egypt to ban the dance altogether. Then as now, the reason was much the same. Scantily clad entertainers who, in the commercial world, are compelled to highlight the more provocative elements of their dance are not a good advertisement for Arab womanhood. Yet their high public profile, in contrast to that of the majority of women in Muslim society, makes them the best known of Arab women outside their own country. Needless to say, at the lower end of the scale, dancers use the cabarets in time-honoured fashion to advertise their charms to potential clients.

Many performers, especially in Europe and America, are now working to raise the level of Arabic dance in the context of clubs and restaurants. Although the cabaret act can be appreciated on its own terms, these terms are largely to do with a fantasy of Oriental dance, Hollywood-style spectacle and show business. This may mean anything from being carried in on a golden litter by four turbaned slaves to sketches parodying the dancers of the notorious Muhammad Ali Street. One of the Arab

Previous page:
Oriental costume, Hollywood style, from 'Intolerance' by D.W. Griffith. 1916. Film still. Museum of Modern Art, New York

Facing page:
Cabaret costume of the 1930s, which has remained largely unchanged to the present day. Photograph. *Arabesque* collection, New York

Egyptian dance goes to Hollywood. 1950s. Film poster. *Arabesque* collection, New York

world's most renowned dancers includes this kind of sketch in her show. She sits at a dressing table and mimes combing her hair, putting on her make-up and applying a deodorant. A besotted admirer later crawls across the stage at her feet while she dances on, ignoring him. Like any entertainment, cabaret can provide moments of sheer enjoyment, but it can also be both boring and embarrassing.

There are many Western performers who have a real love of Arabic dance and believe it can be transformed into a sophisticated theatre art in the cabaret context. Unfortunately, this setting is suitable only for after-dinner diversion. This is partly related to the limited time allowed — the fifteen- or twenty-minute spot into which a dancer has to pack every aspect and mood of the dance. It concerns, too, the ambience of nightclubs and restaurants, and the expectations of most customers who do not go to a club to appreciate good dancing, but in order to see an attractive woman (whose performance skill is more or less immaterial) parading her charms while they digest their dinner.

The attractions of cabaret — regular work and money and a chance to be seen — are hard to resist for any dancer seeking to make a living, but working in cabaret often kills any real love of the dance. The crushing tedium of having to go through the same routine night after night, sometimes to empty tables or to an otherwise occupied audience are only two drawbacks of cabaret life. The audience is there primarily to socialize, and the pressure on a performer to adapt her style in order to catch their attention is unremitting. Even dancers of integrity succumb to the demand of commercialism that their act appeal on the most banal and obvious level. Flashiness, technical expertise rather than feeling and subtlety, and the over-working of the sexual element, have all surfaced in the cabaret act.

Because spectators respond most enthusiastically to the fast, rhythmic elements, these have become prominent in today's highly orchestrated dance music which is too often a busy, gimmicky mixture of international influences. Because the aim is excitement and dazzle, the more lyrical passages are kept to a minimum for fear of boring the audience. Invitations to members of the public to join a performer on stage, constant appeals for applause

Fifi Abdou. 1980s. Photograph.
Arabesque collection, New York

and adulation while in the middle of a number (which may appear to be wonderfully spontaneous) are only two of the affectations of the cabaret act. The central improvisatory role of the dance disappears beneath a choreography so complete that it sometimes extends to an apparently spontaneous interplay with audience and band members alike.

I have, on various occasions, seen performances by one of Egypt's most celebrated dancers which were identical even down to the timing of a moment of humour with a musician and the adjustment of a piece of straying costume. An audience may be charmed by these apparent examples of spontaneity, but they are circus tricks. Arched looks at the audience while lifting the hair from behind, pouting lips, a look of humorous surprise at what a hip is doing, are mannerisms which serve to render the cabaret act more and more banal as they increasingly become part of its stock in trade.

Many performers are perfectly at home in the cabaret world: they accept it for what it is and do not have any particular ambition to extend the boundaries of the dance. The majority are working in clubs and restaurants purely to make money. Among them is a growing number of amateurs with full-time jobs elsewhere, seeking an easy way of earning extra money. A situation has thus developed in which half-trained amateurs are presenting themselves as professional entertainers. Women in the Arab world become dancers because performing is one of the few jobs which enables them to earn a handsome living; they regard the growing number of Western dancers as a particular threat to their livelihood. Why should these women, they reason, who are often highly educated and could easily find work, even work of a different kind, in their own countries, travel all the way to the Middle East to do a job whose conditions are unsatisfactory and difficult? Yet part of cabaret's appeal to Western women as a profession is other than financial and has to do with making a public statement about their sexuality and their identity as women.

For a long time, watching performances in clubs and restaurants, I had a vague feeling of there being an element of the bizarre in the situation. Even though I may have been watching a skilled performer, the individual elements of the dance did not come together as a satisfying whole. There were constant jarring notes; the audience was offered conflicting signals. Lovely moments, passionate moments would be interspersed with stretches of banality and patterns of movement which bore no relation to what had come before or what was to follow. This ill-fitting jigsaw continually jolted the mind with that false offer of intimacy and teasing innuendo which have become such a feature of the cabaret act. If we look at the ancient application of the dance in fertility rites and as a method of choosing a partner, we can see why cabaret dancing is both bizarre and yet oddly compelling. For the cabaret act has developed from this former aspect of the dance. In its original context it had a purpose; it led somewhere. In today's nightclubs and restaurants it leads nowhere. In the impersonal setting of a dimly lit club, the spectacle is that of a woman covered in sequins and rhinestones offering sexual promise to an uninvolved audience of both sexes who think they have gone out for a light-hearted entertainment over supper.

It is form without substance, and it is the inevitable result of commercialism. That is why, when we look round in these places we often find, mingled with looks of enjoyment, so many embarrassed faces. People unfamiliar with the dance are not sure how to respond. There are lowered eyes, frozen smiles, women who look as if they are being threatened and men who are simply confused by the situation. Most Arab men in the audience suspect that a dancer is, by virtue of her profession, disreputable, and that she is simply advertising herself, a conclusion reinforced by the extent of bare flesh on show.

Twenty years ago, in an excellent article about the dance,[74] Professor Morroe Berger pointed out that because of our residue of religious guilt concerning sex, we do not like to glorify it by admitting that it bears any relation to art. Although times may have changed somewhat, there is still an element of truth in this.

Eroticism, like beauty, is in the eye of the beholder, and its expression through dance varies from country to country. As we have seen, legs have long been a focus of the erotic, from the nineteenth-century ballerina 'lifting one leg to the gallery' to the French can-can dancer holding her

Suhair Zaki. 1980s. Photograph. *Arabesque* collection, New York

157

Mae West as a burlesque dancer in 'I'm No Angel'. 1933. Film still. Museum of Modern Art, New York

leg above her head, and the chorus line of the present day. The implied eroticism of Arabic dance is of a different order. It is to do with subtle, insinuating movement of the body, something which those nineteenth-century travellers who insisted on a dancer's appearing nude dismally failed to appreciate.

The erotic image of the female, which in ancient times supported the renewal of life, has become diminished and debased to the extent that in the West today it is loaded with negative connotations. The accepted image of female eroticism, the one which our world finds easiest to handle, is that of the glamorous doll. It is a light image and it is the image of the cabaret act. In this context, it is interesting to recall a remark made of Marilyn Monroe by the actor Robert Mitchum. She once told him that she was amused by her sex goddess image, but that if that was what people wanted her to be, she was happy to oblige. She could not take the image seriously though, he says, and her response was to burlesque it. In her films, she was subtly sending herself up.

In the final analysis, cabaret dancing requires its own particular skills and has its own audience of devotees. But in discussing present and future trends in Arabic dance, it is important to distinguish between this nightclub act and the developing theatre art. At an alternative cabaret in London I once saw a drag artiste perform an Oriental dance. He also did some fire-eating and told a number of hilarious jokes. I enjoyed his dance and its light-hearted parody of female glamour and desirability for it was funny and had no pretensions. The real thing performed by a dancer in deadly earnest as an expression of enticing sexuality does not allow us to laugh, though sometimes that is what we feel like doing. In cabaret the element of parody is not intentional, but it is there all the same, an unconscious travesty of female allure, a cliché which has more to do with a drag act than anything else. It is an interesting reflection of the extent to which only by being thought attractive and sexually alluring do many women feel they have any worth at all.

ENDURING TRADITIONS

In every way Princess Mishaal was an inspired dancer... The language of her movements was infinitely more sophisticated than anything I had ever heard her say.

Rosemarie Buschow, *The Prince and I; Life with the Royal Family of Saudi Arabia*

In the Arab world girls grow up learning to dance from childhood, picking up movements at the innumerable occasions when women get together to relax and amuse themselves. At these informal gatherings, children come to imitate the women's dancing as a matter of course, and are singled out from time to time to show what they can do. In North Africa and the Middle East women sing and dance for each other, with every woman coming forward in turn to entertain her friends. In this situation there is little distinction between performer and spectator, for at different moments everyone will have a chance of being both.

Appreciation is always shown of someone who demonstrates a special skill or grace, and those present will indicate their approval with the *zhagareet*. In Tunisia the *zhagareet* is made by trilling the tongue against the upper palate, in Egypt by fluttering the tongue from side to side while at the same time sounding a continuous, high-pitched note. It is an unearthly sound with a forlorn ring, like the call of a creature from the wild, and it is the particular salutation of women.

While Arabic dance is based on a particular technique, each person develops her own individual style within this framework, unconsciously revealing aspects of her personality as well as her general bearing and spirit. Dance is used above all as a means of self-expression and the customs connected with it serve to enhance its grace and charm. For one thing it is unthinkable that everyone should perform simultaneously, dancing for themselves alone; they come forward as soloists, or in pairs. When someone gets up to dance she always receives the encouragement of her friends, not only before, but during the time that she is dancing. Before

Etienne Dinet. *Children's scarf dance.* 1911. Oil painting. Private collection

159

Learning to dance in Bou Saada.
1890s. Photograph. Private collection

beginning, she ties a scarf round her hips to emphasize the focus of her movements, and when she has finished she may remove her scarf and tie it round the hips of whoever follows her, if they have no scarf of their own. Those sitting around provide musical accompaniment in the form of rhythmic hand-clapping, singing and drumming. The audience is as much a part of the performance as the soloist, and encourages her to give of her best, ululating and hand-clapping and, when especially moved, calling out words of praise such as *Ya lilli ya aini* (You are my eyes), *Ya noori* (You are my light), or *Inti helwa* (How sweet you are).

The dance is a showing rather than a showing off, a showing of the physical self in the best setting of all, an atmosphere of encouragement and appreciation. It is assumed that all of us, rather than the specially gifted few, are dancers; that everyone can do something, even if it is only two or three movements, and that there is no need for a girl to feel embarrassed or inferior if she is not as skilled as her friends.

The ancient custom of a girl dancing to attract a partner survives in modified form in Egypt, where a girl may dance at women's gatherings to show herself off to prospective mothers-in-law. This custom is still current although many middle-class women in North Africa and the Middle East now have a place in public life and are free to socialize with men as they choose.

In some Islamic countries marriages are arranged without the prospective bride and groom knowing each other before their wedding day, although this custom is becoming increasingly rare. A wedding is the most important of all family occasions, a fact reflected in the length of the celebrations, which go on for a minimum of three days, or, if the family finances can run to it, an entire week.

The bride is thought to be especially vulnerable during her transition from girlhood to womanhood, with all manner of spirits, some potentially malevolent, surrounding her at this time. Trance-like dances are used to help banish malevolent spirits, as well as to release negative energies and provide an atmosphere of calm and well-being.

There is an underlying therapeutic element in all Arabic dance: the unleashing of emotion and pent-up energy, the bringing together of people and the showing of the self all have beneficial results. However, most dance is not thought of in terms of therapy. The one exception is trance dancing.

The trance is a therapeutic rite held on behalf of an individual, male or female, who is suffering from problems of a spritual or psychological nature. Their problems may have to do with needs and desires which have failed to find expression in everyday life, or have been deliberately repressed for social reasons. The person afflicted is considered to be suffering from an ailment of the spiritual body and has to go through a process whereby he or she is made whole again, or healed. At a trance ceremony, a woman with clairvoyant powers acts as intermediary between the spirits and the participants. She knows which particular spirit has to be appealed to, and the rhythm needed to call it out, and when she herself is in trance the spirit will talk through her in a voice other than her own. During the ritual, which may go on for hours, even days, musicians strike up rhythms, searching for the one which corresponds to the subject of the ritual, the belief being that every one of us has our own individual spirit rhythm to which we respond instinctively. When the appropriate rhythm is found, the person in question will dance until the point of transcendence is reached, the demons of unease are exorcised and he or she is spiritually cleansed.

The trance dance is not for the eye to appreciate, but for the body's well-being. It is a social dance rather than a theatrical spectacle. It is the duty of everyone around subjects for whom a trance has been called to assist in any way they can, and in particular to reassure them that they are not alone during this time when, discarding their normal defences, they are acutely susceptible to the influences around them. Someone may stand behind them and lightly hold their clothes, linking them with the circle of friends and relatives all around. Afterwards members of the group may help calm the subject, perhaps using a sprinkling of rosewater to bring him or her round.

Trance rituals appear to form a direct link with the fertility dances of the ancient world. In 1920 Joseph McPherson, an English teacher and later head of the secret police in Egypt, witnessed a *zaar*

The duet. 1890s. Photograph. Private collection

ceremony in a house on the outskirts of Cairo. It is extremely unusual for an outsider, in particular a man from a foreign country, to gain admittance to this highly secret ceremony, and McPherson's account is especially interesting for this reason alone. He describes the initial stages of the *zaar* during which, to the accompaniment of drumming, the women sang a song which, he commented:

> was nothing Quranic, Islamic or religious. I had heard nothing like it previously in Egypt. [The song made] repeated reference to the sacrifice of a beautiful youth whose blood became a flower... I felt sure that the *zaar* must be an important institution, dating back to the Grecian mysteries, or to the cults of Baal and Tammuz.[75]

As the excitement of the ceremony mounted, the women rose to their feet and danced around an altar on which stood baskets of flowers, fruit and nuts, together with lighted candles, one of them four foot in length. When the passion was at its height, the women fell to the ground and there was a dramatic silence. The animals, a ram, two ganders and a pair of red doves and rabbits, were then slaughtered and their blood collected in a large basin and placed on the altar, to the accompaniment of chanting and the burning of incense. The *aalima* (leader of the ceremony) then thrust her arms and hands into the blood, mingled it and smeared it on the faces and robes of herself and the other initiates.

> It seemed to have a magic effect, for their previous frenzy had been cold compared with the mad fury which now possessed them. Their hair was torn down by bloody fingers and their gestures and cries were frantic... Sometimes they bent their bodies back till they formed a vibrating and writhing bow, resting on the ground by the heels and back of the head, whilst the muscles of their bodies carried on the dance with unbelievable contortions... many of the women in the Bacchanalian frenzy were pulling from their bosoms, and holding carefully concealed in their hands as they danced, some little objects which I in vain tried to get an adequate glimpse of.[76]

The women then proceeded to sing songs which, McPherson comments, were 'erotic and, in keeping, their dancing became indecent'. At this point he was persuaded to leave.

The trance rituals of today found in various countries of North Africa and the Middle East take different forms and may not be of a similar intensity to that witnessed by McPherson; however, many of the customs connected with them are similar. The sacrifice of an animal during, or at the start of, a trance ceremony continues to be observed. Out of respect for the jinn or spirits, and also to close herself off from outside influence, the dancer covers her face and head. Then, as she begins to respond to the rhythm and the trance comes, she discards the veil and abandons herself to the power which has been unleashed from within.

Every element of a trance ceremony is important, from the incense used at the beginning to calm and welcome the spirits, to the colours of the clothes worn. Black represents the earth spirit, white the air, red is for fire and blue for water. In Egypt this ceremony is called the *zaar*; in Algeria, *gargabous*; in Tunisia, *stambali*; and in Morocco it is the dance of the Gnaouias, a people from the southern Sahara. Trance-like dances are not only performed to assuage illness. Since the main purpose of this type of dance is to release negative energies, it may also be used if a woman feels she has been unlucky in some way — if, for example, she has been unsuccessful in conceiving a child. At weddings, trance-like dances of lesser intensity often form part of the women's celebrations, to calm the spirits and create positive energies around the bride.

In many Arab countries, where men and women celebrate in separate quarters of the house, the women dance privately for each other while the men either do the same or else hire a troupe of professional musicians and dancers to entertain them. At a wedding in Marrakesh, I was invited to go and watch these professional dancers. My companion and I were first offered a meal in an adjoining room, with four or five of the men. Plates heaped with food, giving off a delicious scent of aromatic herbs and spices, were brought in and set before us on the low brass table — dishes of chicken with rice and baked fruits, warm bread and *tagine*

Persian wedding party.
Qajar dynasty,
early 19th century.
Oil painting.
Victoria & Albert Museum,
London

(a casserole of meat and vegetables). With torn-off pieces of bread, the men reached into the communal bowl in the middle of the table and pushed the choicest chunks of meat towards me and my companion. This savoury feast was followed by cakes fresh from the oven, soaked in honey which dripped in long, warm streams into the bowl from which we helped ourselves with our sticky fingers. One of the women brought in bowls of water and towels for our hands, and as we entered the men's room a young girl sprinkled us with orange-flower water.

The men were sitting on low benches and cushions around the blue and white tiled walls. The troupe was a local one. A *rababa* player sat cross-legged on the floor, playing his instrument (a precursor of today's fiddle) much like a cello, holding it upright on the floor. The *rababa* is a two-stringed instrument with a coconut-shell body and is often found in small folk-music ensembles. Two drummers sat beside the *rababa* players, holding up their goatskin-covered *bendirs*, sieve-like drums which are played with the fingers and palms of one hand.

A dancer came forward. She wore a heavy brocade dress which covered her from throat to ankle, caught in at the waist with a black woollen belt plaited with silver sequins. Her hair was hidden beneath a headscarf wound round her head and tied in a large knot on top. She took up a tray containing nine or ten glasses with lighted candles in them, and placed it on her head. Holding her arms aloft, her hands curled up into fists, she made her stomach appear to jump up and down. She knelt on the floor and stretched herself out on the carpet, the candles flickering in their glasses, the tray tilting precariously on the crown of her head. I was aware of a whispering, a soft rustling just above my head. I glanced up at the balcony running all around the room and saw, half-hidden behind the dark wooden bannisters, the brilliant pink, green and silver of the women's clothes. The children and young girls had come silently out of their room to catch a glimpse of the professional dancers. Just as the women are not allowed to mingle with the male guests, so too are the men banned from witnessing the private entertainments of the women. Even in a liberal country like Egypt, men and women tend to

Facing page:
Muhammad Racim. *Wedding celebrations in Algeria*. c.1830. Miniature

celebrate separately, as has been my experience at weddings in the villages of the Sa'id (the south). In those Muslim countries where women have either a limited or non-existent role in public life, dancing is one of the principal means of expression and self-affirmation.

As we have seen, separate development in the harem and the obligatory use of the veil are characteristic of strict Islamic societies. In these societies, a woman's honour, her most important gift, can only be upheld by never submitting it to any kind of temptation; she can only maintain her integrity by concealing herself and leading the life of a protected object. Once again we find ourselves confronting the pervasive concept of women's irresistible, disruptive powers of attraction.

It has been said that, while women in these societies have no choice in the question of veiling, they are none the less able to use the veil to their own advantage, in that it allows them to move about in public in complete anonymity. However, it must be stressed that the obligation to veil is not synonymous with the free decision to do so. Cultural anthropologist S. Deaver, writing about the lives of Saudi women,[77] comments on the contrast between their public and private demeanour: their public concealment by means of the veil, and their private display, through extravagant dress and entertainment and where the only male members of the household present are pre-pubescent boys. One motive behind this private entertainment, she writes, is the affirmation of a woman's beauty and sexual appeal. The message she conveys through her dancing is that she is secure, that she has all the attributes necessary to keep her husband: 'By displaying her status within her own peer group, a female displays her wealth and continued ability to attract a man — the source of wealth.'

So acute are the strictures concerning women's lives in Saudi Arabia that Deaver was prevented from taking photographs at a women's party for fear the pictures might fall into the hands of the men. She only once observed an unmarried girl performing at these private gatherings, and 'She was not regarded by the audience as a serious participant. Rather, she was regarded as a child playing at an adult exercise.'

Algerian dancer Amel Benhassine-Miller, who teaches bedouin dance in London, has commented on the way in which the dance reflects the close-knit intensity of the women's community rather than its serious, competitive element. Bedouin dance, with its emphasis on the group, is a particular expression of this closeness. Women improvise in pairs, matching each other's movements. In work dances a woman comes out of a line of dancers to improvise, but she is always part of the whole; rarely is she a soloist for very long.

Dancing is not considered the unique province of the young. It is the expression, rather, of a woman's entire life experience, whether it is used as a symbol of luck and fertility, an aid to childbirth, a means of passing the time, a form of therapy or a means of helping the work go quicker. And though the older women may well confine themselves to dispensing refreshments, leaving the dancing to the young girls, those well past their youth sometimes prove to be the most exciting performers at these private gatherings, for their dance is invested with the grace notes of maturity and fullness.

The Arab ideal of female beauty does not confine itself to the young and slim, but also takes in the quality of the voluptuous, with its hint of an enveloping protectiveness and sensual ease. Some years ago I was sitting with a Moroccan friend in a little café near Fez. It was run by a woman whom I would guess was in her late forties, a woman of ample, generous proportions. My friend could not take his eyes off her. 'See how beautiful she is,' he said, and when I did not immediately echo his enthusiasm, he went on more emphatically, 'She is truly beautiful. And this woman is a wonderful dancer. Wait. You'll see.'

Several of the young men in the café pressed her to dance, but she only laughed and shrugged them off as if they were tiresome schoolboys. Finally, she left her seat by the counter and, more to humour them than for any other reason, I thought, began dancing in the confined space between the tables. With her plump white arms held aloft and her swaying hips, she made me think of a galleon in full sail. She used her weight to reinforce the heavy, earthy quality of the dance, centring her movement low in the abdomen, her feet lightly brushing the floor.

It was not an isolated case of a large woman of mature years dancing magnificently. She was the same age as some of the most celebrated professional performers in the Arab world today. Arab dancers need not fear their dancing days are over at 40, or even 50. Their long prime reflects the unique possibilities of this dance, whose scope is enriched rather than narrowed by age, and whose continuing importance in everyday life is a testament to all that it has to offer.

A MOSAIC OF MUSIC

Chapter 9

*These frail, quavering melodies resound like the
whispering of solitude, like the voices of the wilderness
that speak to the soul lost in contemplation of space;
they stir a strange nostalgia, dredge up infinite
memories and conjure forth previous lives that come
straying back in random array.*

Théophile Gautier

Arabic dance is shaped by its accompanying music.
This music is never simply background, it is
composed around the dance. Yet while it is a vehicle
for the dancer, the opposite is also true: a dancer
is responsible for the direction taken by the music.
Musicians follow a dancer, giving her the particular
rhythms and moods she requires. Meanwhile, it is
her task to express the emotions called forth by the
music and, during improvisations around a solo
instrument, to bring out that instrument's essential
quality. A dancer and her musicians cue each other
in unobtrusive ways, to continue or come to an end
of a passage in the music, and when she and her
band have a good rapport the result can be
enthralling, with each performer spurring the others
on to moments of shared invention and humour.

The term 'Arabic' music is misleading. Notes,
rhythms, instruments and singing styles vary from
country to country. Yet all Arabic music shares
certain similarities. One of these is that, within its
formal structure, it has retained from the past a
strong improvisatory quality; another is that it is
primarily melodic. Unlike Western music, it has not
developed the use of harmony. The basic reason is
that harmony depends on a fixed tonal system (an
unvarying space between notes). Every scale in
Arabic music has certain fixed positions (tones and
half tones), as in Western music, but in between
them are notes which have no fixed place and fall in
slightly different positions in a scale each time they
are played. In Arabic music a single octave (eight
equally distanced notes in Western music) may
contain anything between eighteen and twenty-two

notes, with intervals as fine as a ninth of a tone. The only compositions which can include simple harmonies are those based on a Western melody and scale. It is these which we sometimes hear in modern orchestral recordings. Within the elaborate scale system of Arabic music, instrumentalists have room to explore a melody, rather in the manner of a jazz improvisation. This is done by taking the melody and weaving complex patterns around it, in the same way that Islamic art takes a central motif and ornaments it with a pattern of arabesques.

The closest approximation to the oldest Arabic music can be found in the Arab-Andalusian mode, a style of the Maghreb. The Moors, Europe's term for successive arrivals of Arab and Berber peoples, were in Spain for 700 years. They initially conquered al-Andalus, as they christened it, at the beginning of the eighth century, and for a while it remained no more than a remote province of the growing Islamic empire. Yet in time al-Andalus, which embraced more than the area covered by present-day Andalusia, became the major channel of Islamic civilization to the West. In AD 750 the Umayyad dynasty was overthrown in Damascus and established itself in Andalusia. The culture-loving Umayyads brought the ancient music of eastern Arabia to Spain, where it was later modified by Greek influences and became the Arab-Andalusian music which took root in North Africa.

In 822 the musician Ziryab arrived in Spain from the Abbasid court of Baghdad, bringing with him Persian musical forms which have survived in Andalusia and still linger on in flamenco. The first conservatory of music was founded in the twelfth century in Cordoba, at that time one of the most celebrated cultural centres of Europe. By then the majority of Andalusians spoke Arabic and had come to embrace Islam. Islam's domination of Spain lasted until the eleventh century, when the unity of the Caliphate gave way to ethnic and tribal divisions, with the Muslims finally being ousted from Europe in 1492.

The inter-penetration of artistic styles in Moorish Spain has left more than splendid architectural monuments behind it. In feeling, tempo and lilt, the music of Spain is more Arab than European. Flamenco is a mixture of Moorish, Andalusian and

Facing page:
Filippo Bartolini. *The courtyard.*
c.1860. Oil painting. Mathaf Gallery, London

Following page:
Persian oud player. Qajar dynasty, early 18th century. Oil panel. Victoria & Albert Museum, London

gypsy elements, and in its earliest form is particularly Arab in flavour, with rhythms separated by slight pauses. This is a feature of both songs and instrumental compositions.

The principal instrument of flamenco, the guitar, developed out of the *oud*, the classical instrument of Arabic music. The *oud*, which provides both melody and rhythm, is the prototype on which Arab musical theory is based and has been celebrated by many Arab poets. It is hollowed out of a single block of wood, and it was once believed that, when the wood was still part of a tree, the singing of birds perching on its branches gave it its resonance, which was then transferred to the instrument from which it was made. Through Moorish Spain, the *oud* found its way to the rest of Europe, developing first into a lute and then into today's guitar.

To examine the music of all Arab countries would take a book in itself. I have chosen to concentrate on the Middle Eastern style, exemplified by the music of Egypt, which has absorbed most changes over the years and is most closely connected with the women's solo dance. Middle Eastern music encompasses many traditions, including that of Iraq, Egypt and the Fertile Crescent.

It is difficult to distinguish between classical and popular styles. Musicians do not talk in terms of a special court music or an independent style which goes back to antiquity, though many mention the Andalusian style of North Africa as the one that best shows its roots. Classical music is a refinement of the folk tradition. The least sophisticated, or folk, music of North Africa and the Middle East is that which accompanies traditional dancing such as that of the Moroccan *chikhat* and the Egyptian *ghawazee*.

When women get together informally to entertain each other they make music by singing, rhythmic hand-clapping and drumming, using the *bendir* and its Middle Eastern equivalent, the *daff*. Contra-rhythms are set up, using different types of clapping: hollowing the hands produces a dark sound, for example, while slapping the fingers against the palms results in a sharper, clearer note. This complicated hand-clapping is a special feature of North African music. The only drum played with sticks, rather than the hands, is the *tabl baladi*, a huge two-sided kettledrum hanging from a strap round the neck. Its

Clément Pujol. *Entertaining the Shaikh.* 19th century. Oil painting. Mathaf Gallery, London

---

Egyptian musicians with mazhar player, far right. Mid-19th century. Tinted lithograph. Private collection

Alex Bida. *Tabla player*. c.1850.
Colour lithograph. Victoria & Albert
Museum, London

Facing page:
*Persian dancer making the beshkan
(finger snap)*. Qajar dynasty, early
19th century. Oil painting. Tehran
Ethnological Museum

deep, heavy sound makes it a popular instrument for processional celebrations such as weddings and religious ceremonies.

The most popular rhythm instruments of both folk and classical music are the *darabouka* (North Africa) and the *tabla* (Egypt), large, goblet-shaped drums covered in fish-skin which produce a deep sound and, in the hands of a skilled player, the most subtle embellishments, using the palms and fingers.

The highly developed rhythmic element in music accompanying today's classical dance, *sharqi*, is a fairly recent development, though there is a long tradition in Egypt and Turkey of dancers using finger cymbals to provide their own rhythms or augment the percussive element in the music. The Indian gypsy Kathaka used *klavos*, two pairs of wooden sticks, later modified to a rounded shape and linked by a cord. Old illustrations of Turkish and Persian dancers show them manipulating wooden clappers very like these *klavos*, while today's flamenco still uses wooden castanets. They are, however, often disdained by gypsies, who refer to them as 'false finger snaps'. This finger snap is still a feature of north Persian dance: a performer lifts her arms above her head and, placing her palms together and linking the index fingers in a particular way, produces a surprisingly loud and penetrating clicking sound. *Sagat*, or finger cymbals, are used today during the festive opening of a dance. At weddings, the bride is 'cymballed in' by a dancer who enters slightly ahead of her, attracting the guests' attention with this delicate, tinkling fanfare. In cabarets, when a dancer goes round the tables at the end of her act, she may use them to 'speak' for her, asking for tips.

Modern Middle Eastern music has been influenced in various ways by the West, ways which are sometimes welcomed, sometimes not. In the Yemen, musicians who play traditional melodies are well respected, while those who emulate a Western style are held in contempt. Conversely, in Egypt and Lebanon Western music has been accepted for the diversity it offers. Western influence on Egyptian music stems from late-nineteenth century attempts to modernize the country, as well as the later impact of the mass media. This impact was concentrated in the major cities; thus we speak not of classical and popular Egyptian styles, but of *baladi* (country or folk) and urban secular music.

From the late nineteenth century onwards, new melodic modes, metric patterns and types of composition were assimilated into the music of Egypt, while the type of instruments used in an ensemble changed and grew in variety. The *tabla*, originally a *baladi* instrument, became prominent in ensembles only after the First World War. The traditional group of four or five instruments grew to a full-scale orchestra; European-style military bands resulted in the gradual addition of brass, while the violin, electric organ, accordian, double bass and cello gradually became an accepted part of an Egyptian ensemble.

The greater the number and variety of instruments, the easier it is to create a sustained sound. As a band grew from five or six members to the orchestras of today, so the music took on a richer texture, with particular instruments or groups of instruments dominating certain passages in the music. More percussionists made for a more complex ornamentation of rhythms, and a music which in the past had been principally improvisatory took on a more highly structured form.

The result of this growing complexity can be seen in the *taqasim*, which occur several times during a long composition. *Taqasim* (sing. *taqsim*) are instrumental solos which connect the various melodies of an extended piece and serve as an interlude between them. During the *taqasim* an instrumentalist comes forward (metaphorically

speaking) to improvise, while the others either lay down their instruments or else take a back seat, very much in the manner of a jazz improvisation. For example, a steady background drone on a violin or other bowed instrument can provide support for the husky, plaintive notes of the *nai* (a bamboo flute), one of the most evocative instruments in Arabic music.

It is said that when al-Mahdi, one of the last caliphs of Cordoba, entertained, the sound of a hundred flutes and a hundred lutes filled the air. The *nai* has a plaintive, yearning quality which can send shivers down the spine. The more meditative, spiritual elements in the dance are often inspired by this instrument, using languorous movements of the arms and upper torso. Within an extended piece of music there are generally three or four *taqasim*, on *nai*, *oud*, violin and *kanoon*.

The *kanoon* is a predecessor of the harp and piano and is played with finger plectrums, a tradition which, it has been suggested, may derive from playing it in former times with long fingernails. It sets up a shimmering vibration in the air which prompts intense, trembling movements in the dance. A *taqsim* begins by exploring a few notes, gradually widening this range of notes to create a kaleidoscope of sound. A 'pulse' or understated rhythm may then be brought in to support the solo instrument while the *taqsim* builds to a higher key. It then embroiders patterns which wind down progressively to an ending in the original key. One purpose of a *taqsim* may be to change the key for the following melody; thus it will end on this new key. A musician's skill is judged by how many scales he or she can explore during a single *taqsim* before returning to the scale in which the improvisation began.

Taqasim are linked, like pearls on a chain, by rhythmic passages in which the entire band unites, as if to chorus an agreement of what the solo instrument has just been saying. *Taqasim* are generally non-metric and are never played in a similar fashion twice. Pauses, or breaths, between each extended phrase give the audience a chance to express its appreciation of a player's skill, and I have heard exclamations of near ecstasy on the part of the audience (the common cry *Y'Allah!* — Oh God! — is the origin of the Spanish *Olé!*).

Facing page, top:
Levni. *Turkish cengi using wooden finger clappers.* 18th century. Miniature. Topkapi Palace Museum, Istanbul

Facing page, bottom:
Leichenstein and Harari. *Café entertainers, Egypt* (instruments, left to right, are: *sagat, reque* and *daff*). 1890s. Postcard. Private collection

179

'To some people music is meat, to others it is medicine,' runs an old Arab proverb. Music traditionally holds a special place in Arab life, and there are many treatises devoted to musical theory. A singing girl was once as common a part of any moderately comfortable Arab household as was a piano in Victorian England.

In the Middle Ages particular *maqamat* (scales) were associated with the signs of the zodiac; certain *maqamat* were also believed to have a therapeutic influence and were associated with particular mental states.

During the rise of the Caliphate, musicians had a place in court life from Persia to Spain. None the less, Islam was predictably ambivalent towards music. While accepting its devotional element it condemned its more frivolous aspect, which was a potentially distracting force in that it lured the mind from a proper state of religious contemplation. While the Quran does not condemn music, certain sayings attributed to Muhammad were antithetical to it. Following the death of the Prophet, successive caliphs issued warnings against its influence:

> It lessens modesty, increases lust and saps virility. It is indeed like wine, and does what strong drink does. If you must have it, at least keep your women from it, song being such a spur to lechery.[78]

Before the advent of Islam, music was dominated by women to such an extent that men who sought to enter the profession were dubbed effeminate. Coincident with the seclusion of women in the harem, male musicians emerged on the scene, mimicking women's ways, even down to wearing female clothing and dyeing their hands with henna. They became known as *mukhannath* (effeminate) and though the best known of them, 'the little peacock', earned the title of 'the father of song', he was none the less expelled from the holy city of Medina because of his profession.

The Umayyads instituted musical entertainment as part of court life in Damascus. They were roundly criticized for their patronage of the arts, especially music, which was considered an idolatrous rival of the Quran because of the spiritual fervour which it

Facing page:
Turkish kanoon player. 1714. Etching on stipple, after J.B. Van Mour. Victoria & Albert Museum, London

Following page:
Muhammad Racim. *Evening in Algiers*. 1832. Miniature

was capable of arousing. Their successors, the Abbasids, maintained the tradition of music as a more discreet feature of court life, enjoying it in private, in the company of their most intimate companions. The Abbasid caliph al-Mahdi was a well-known patron of the art, yet when he learnt that one of his musicians came from a noble family he did not fail to reprimand him: 'You... One of the Quraish, and following the profession of music! What a disgrace!'

Music is an art which conjures up mood and memory like no other. The fear that, because of its power, it encourages people to lose self-control and indulge in all kinds of unacceptable practices, has frequently caused it to be banned in Muslim fundamentalist countries.

Many nineteenth-century travellers commented on the hypnotic quality of Arabic music. At first, to their unaccustomed ear, it sounded repetitive; only later, on closer acquaintance, did they come to appreciate it. As Charles de Carcy commented:

> It surprises; it begins by assailing the ears of the listener, then one becomes accustomed to it; one listens without tiring of it; and finally it brings on a kind of drowsiness or trance state, which is not unpleasant, and against which one has neither the power nor the will to resist.[79]

To appreciate Arabic music one must abandon the Western expectation that it be full of obvious change and variety. The change and variety are there, but they are very subtle. The music's hypnotic effect has been compared to that of waves breaking on a shore. It is an apt comparison, for no two waves ever break in the same way twice, nor is their sound exactly alike. The more we listen to Arabic music, the more we are able to discern its subtle nuances.

Interest in ethnic music, a legacy of the sixties which has largely concentrated on Africa and to a lesser extent India, has recently turned its attention to the Arab world. Many Western musicians are discovering Arab rhythms and musical modes, and their collaboration with North African and Middle Eastern musicians is producing an interesting fusion of these diverse musical traditions.

It is sometimes objected that this kind of experimentation results in a loss of musical purity.

Edmund Dulac. *A musical entertainment, from the 'Tales of 1001 Nights'.* Book illustration

Persian musician. 1841. Etching after Louis Dubeux. Victoria & Albert Museum, London

183

But how is this purity to be evaluated? The gypsies who left India, crossed the Arab world and entered Spain in the fifteenth century left intriguing mementoes of their passing in the music of these culturally diverse lands. Their principal contribution to local folk music was the development of complex rhythm, the ornamentation of melody and a preference for a minor musical key. All these are central characteristics of Arabic music. So, we may ask, would North African and Middle Eastern music have developed as it has without absorbing the innovations brought by gypsies from other lands?

There is always the possibility that, in a bid for popular success, ill-fitting elements from the Western tradition will be woven into Arabic music to make it more accessible to a Western audience. Modern Egyptian music, with its international influences and heavy orchestration, has gone furthest in the hybridization of Arabic music.

Like all the arts, music retains its vitality and freshness by taking inspiration from the sources around it. Whether it be the innovations of gypsies hundreds of years ago or the popular music of today, both contribute in their own way to the rich mosaic of a living musical tradition.

Persian musician. 1841. Etching after Louis Dubeux. Victoria & Albert Museum, London

Chapter 10

NEW DIRECTIONS

It was the suppleness of the serpent joined to the grace of the gazelle.

Paul Lenoir

I once gave a performance with a Tunisian dancer who presented a trance dance as one of her solos. At the London art gallery where we were appearing, I stood backstage and watched her perform a Moroccan dance of the Gnaouias. I noticed that an Iranian friend of mine was picking his way through the audience towards the stage. The floor was packed with people sitting cross-legged on cushions and rugs, and it was no easy matter to penetrate such a crowd. Was he intending to join in? I didn't think it likely, even though, among Middle Eastern audiences, if people are especially moved by a performance, they may well jump up and join a dancer on stage.

The music ended and the Tunisian dancer came through the curtain, gasping: 'I nearly went into trance then. I only just stopped myself.' My Iranian friend later told us he could see how near she was to this point and was coming forward so that he would be on hand to help her, if needed. When a trance ritual is part of a theatre programme, a performer cannot abandon herself completely to the dance; she has to keep part of her mind alert and in control of the situation. Trance dancing is a rite for the body rather than the eye, and some performers believe it has no place in a theatre programme. When it is presented in this setting, only a fragment of it can be shown. It is a speeded-up version of the stages through which someone passes in the journey of self-abandonment, yet even the briefest example is enough to indicate the overwhelming power of this ritual.

Some performers include an example of a trance, together with other social dances, to demonstrate the diversity of Arabic dance. Others intersperse dance with short stories, anecdotes and poems, in order to inform Western audiences about the life

Monika Kaiblinger. *Dancer from Tangier*. 1986. Oil painting. Private collection

and customs of the Islamic world. As a theatre art, Arabic dance has yet to reach maturity; it is still in the process of being defined.

At one end of the professional scale we find bedouin and other folk dance troupes such as the *ghawazee* and the *chikhat*, who entertain at family festivities in towns and villages. This kind of entertainment is largely spontaneous and casual; it is relatively simple and almost wholly improvised. At the other end of the spectrum we find the polished, highly choreographed work of government-sponsored troupes and independent soloists.

Essentially an intimate mode of expression, Arabic dance does not lend itself to an impersonal setting. As times change and interest in it grows, however, it is increasingly being presented in formal settings where, in the West at least, audiences do not respond with the verve which frequently greets the dance in its own cultural context. For this restrained and critical public, seated in formal rows in darkened theatres, it is necessary to re-evaluate every aspect of the dance: its costuming, the length and type of numbers on a programme, as well as its potential as a narrative art.

In the professional field, there are many directions in which Arabic dance is being taken today. Government-sponsored companies such as Lebanon's Caracalla and Egypt's Reda Troupe concentrate primarily on group and folk dance, developing their humorous and story-telling potential. Performers working in Europe and America, on the other hand, tend to concentrate on refining and extending the boundaries of the solos, *baladi* and *sharqi*, even using them to create choreographed group dances.

The development of Arabic dance as a theatre art has achieved its greatest sophistication so far in the solo. Over the years *baladi* has evolved a technique suited to the confined performance conditions in which it grew up, and in which it was seen until fairly recently. Even today, when performers of *baladi* have a large stage at their disposal, they concentrate not on travelling across the floor, but on making intense and intricate movements of the lower torso and hips, while standing in place with the arms casually lifted and held. In *baladi* a dancer presents a movement or pose to different members of her audience in turn, an audience which is generally sitting all around her. Even if the spectators are only on one side, she still presents side and back views of a dance pattern to them.

Unlike ballet — a finished product designed for an impersonal audience — *baladi* has developed out of a dancer's contact with her audience and musicians, and for this reason alone is never fully choreographed. Even so, a professional dancer must have in mind the creation of a tableau or picture, using sets of movements which correspond to the different stages over which a piece of music may range. Each picture, while linked to the others, is as self-sufficient and important in the scheme as its neighbours.

The patterning of a dance may be compared to that of an Oriental carpet in which each individual design has its own beauty, its own special quality. When we look at this kind of carpet we do not focus

Amel Benhassine-Miller and Dawson Miller in an Algerian trance dance. 1988. Photograph. Private collection

only on a single central figure. So it is with the dance. Each passage reaches a resolution, or climax, of its own rather than building to a single, all-important resolution. Sometimes a dancer may not even come to a final ending, but will continue her movement as she exits, leaving us to carry on the dance in our own imagination. Again like an Oriental carpet, whose design continues into the borders, the implication is that there is no end to the pattern; it may go on and on, duplicating itself in untold ways.

Comparing *baladi* to this type of ornamental art reveals that while the women's dance has often been condemned by Islamic fundamentalists it has, over the years, evolved in ways which harmonize closely with the abstract, stylized nature of Islamic art in general. A tradition in which no natural object has served as model, its geometric motifs and flowing arabesques evoke above all a feeling of contemplation and calm. They rest the eye and soothe the mind, rather than distract it. One of the basic characteristics of *baladi* is just this sense of quiet which it provokes in an audience. Its essence is inner rhythm and repose, a balance of restraint and abandon.

Gobineau commented on its mesmerizing effect and 'hypnotic intoxication'. He added, 'Its repetitive nature and unchanging rhythms exhale a delightful torpor upon the soul.' A hundred years ago, when Gobineau was writing down his impressions, the dance was perhaps less complex than it is today. It is just as likely, though, that he missed its subtleties for, like a series of arabesques, the intricate detail of a dance pattern is perceived only on close examination. A performer may send a wave of motion rippling up and down her torso until it comes to rest in the hips. As it sinks into the pelvis it becomes a horizontal movement, tracing undulatory designs around the hips — circular, looping figures weaving in and out of each other with wave-like fluidity. And so a pattern develops, moving smoothly up and down the body until the music changes and a new mood, a new type of movement is needed. As this change occurs a dancer may pause, creating a moment of absolute stillness, a frame for a completed design, before moving on to the next. At such a moment there is a certain suspense: the eye of the spectator is rested, yet the mind is alert, anticipating what may follow.

Recurrent patterns of movement create unity in a dance but their order, together with the combination of steps used, differs according to a performer's individual style. A gifted dancer creates her own movements to add to *baladi*'s basic technical repertoire. She has the ability to spontaneously adapt and improvise according to the needs of the occasion, especially those of space (which may not accommodate her choreography) and the idiosyncracies of her musicians, on whom she is particularly dependent.

Working together over a long period of time, musicians come to know a dancer's style and anticipate her movements, as well as the rhythm and tempi she will require. A professional dancer finds it difficult to perform with a band she has never met before. They do not know her style and she has to be particularly alert to theirs. If things are not going well, she will use the informal element always present in the dance to pause at the end of a section in the music and make it clear to her musicians what she wants. All this is done unobtrusively, without the audience being aware of any negotiations taking place between the performers.

Travel writers have given us a vivid picture of *baladi* from the eighteenth to the early twentieth century. The late nineteenth century may well have been a time when it came to a particular flowering. For, as we have seen, from then onwards, when Arab performers came to Europe and America and began adding outside elements to their dance, the fundamental feel of *baladi* began to change.

With this change came a separation of styles, a new branch issuing from the main stem of the dance. On the one hand *baladi* retained its traditional look and feel, changing largely to accommodate developments in the music over the years. On the other hand it branched off in a radically new direction and a fresh style was created, today's *raks al-sharqi*. These two forms differ from each other in interesting ways.

The music for *baladi* resonates low in the body, placing the dance's centre of movement firmly in the hips. Rolling, undulating and shimmering movements

predominate, with casual arms and heavy elbows. Performed on the flat or balls of the feet, *baladi* has a heavy, grounded look. It also has a certain poignancy which relates to the general theme of its accompanying music — that of suffering and disappointed love. Developed in the towns and cities of today, it contains an element of melancholy which owes something to the loss of an agrarian tradition and the problems of urban life. It is a dance of earthy sexuality with a take-it-or-leave-it air, and is very womanly. In the words of Egyptian musician Hossam Ramzy, it has 'all the enticement of the ghetto'. Its accompanying music is dominated by the accordian or electric organ, with an underlying percussive element. Today's *baladi*, which is continually being modified, differs from town to town and village to village in Egypt.

Sharqi, the hybrid which has developed out of *baladi*, has been influenced by diverse dance traditions. Elements of Indian, Persian and Turkish dance can all be found in *sharqi*, which is sometimes known as the classical style, implying that it is the most refined and sophisticated dance of the Arab world. The Asiatic influence on *sharqi* can be seen in its poise and dignity; from India and Persia it has taken head, hand and arm movements and from Turkey its supple, undulating spine.

In addition to these motley influences, *sharqi* has come to assimilate a number of Western elements. The earliest exponent of this style on film is Samia Gamal, who can be seen in Egyptian movies of the thirties, incorporating in her dance balletic turns, soaring arm movements and an entrance using a diaphanous veil. Today it has become a feature of *sharqi* to open a dance with this veil. When used with imagination and skill, this brings an added dimension to the classical style, heightening the audience's perception of the energy flow around the upper torso and above the head.

Sharqi's centre of movement is in the upper torso rather than the hips. With its lifted spine and graceful arms held high above the head, *sharqi* coincides with the balletic ideal of soaring movement and the beauty of extended line. It is danced on the balls of the feet, rather than the flat, and is rooted in rhythm. The *tabla* provides a basic structure for the music and sets the body in motion, driving the hips while the

190

melody weaves its way around this basic, stabilizing beat.

It is a long dance, lasting anything from fifteen to thirty minutes, in which various songs and melodies are strung together in such a way as to offer a dancer the chance to display *sharqi*'s rich repertoire. A typical *sharqi* composition consists of an upbeat opening and a series of melodies linked by three or four *taqasim*, on *oud, nai, kanoon* and violin. During the *taqasim* a dancer seeks to express the emotions called forth by each of these instruments in turn.

I remember a dancer once commenting that the sound of the *nai*, with its alternately silvery and husky notes, made her think of a snake; hence she tried to produce the movement of a snake. A *nai taqsim* often explores movements of arms, shoulders and upper torso, and expresses the more spiritual aspects of the dance. The *kanoon*, an instrument which produces tones of a shimmering vibration, prompts an intense trembling of the muscles, most commonly in the hips, though this movement can be extended to the entire torso.

The *taqasim* are followed by a drum solo with *tabla* prominent. This is one of the most popular parts of a dance for the audience, which responds instinctively to the hard-hitting, playful rhythms. The drum solo is outgoing and bold, and if a dancer has a good rapport with her *tabla* player it can be the most enjoyable part of the dance for her. When the audience is clapping along and the music is good, she can be inspired by their support and feedback to bring out that aspect of the dance which is uniquely concerned with sharing its humour and playfulness directly with the audience. The *tabla* solo is the final climax in a series of dance climaxes and is followed by an upbeat, closing melody in which the entire band joins, ending in a triumphant flourish.

To the general public dance is not interesting to watch for long periods at a time. Many people who would not think twice about going to a film or play would hesitate to struggle with the foreign language of dance movement as an idea of a night out. Yet it is as true today as it was 200 years ago that people are entranced by Arabic dance when they encounter it for the first time. Even those who are not especially interested in dance come back time and again to enjoy it.

Jawad Selim. *Dancer.* c.1950. Watercolour. Private collection

Facing page:
Chiparus. *Dourga.* c.1930. Bronze and ivory figure. Private collection

Dancer of the Ouled Nail. c.1930.
Bronze figure. Private collection

When presented as a theatre art, however, certain of its essential qualities have to be sacrificed. In the context of an intimate gathering, a wedding or an informal get-together in which there are other points of interest, the repetitive nature of folk dancing and its limited repertoire of movements are unimportant. In a darkened auditorium, however, the dance is all. In order to hold the audience's attention part of its improvisatory element must be sacrificed, together with certain subtleties of movement which a Western audience unaccustomed to the dance will not appreciate simply because they will not notice them. In this situation, choreography and variety become especially important.

When channelling what is essentially a spontaneous folk art in the direction of choreography and identical costuming, there is always a danger of losing the spirit of the original. A balance between repetition and variety, story-telling and self-expression is perhaps the most difficult task faced by those who seek to translate Arabic dance for a theatre audience into programmes an hour and a half or more in length.

The same may be said concerning the balance between virtuosity and warmth. An Arab audience values passion and feeling just as highly as virtuosity, whereas a Western audience tends to look for technical expertise. Yet while it is essential to master the vocabulary of the dance, neither *baladi* nor *sharqi* nor any of the folk dances are only 'about' technique.

Dazzling virtuosity may impress us, yet if a performer is merely interested in showing off her technical brilliance her performance leaves us cold. It is like being shown an exquisite flower with no perfume. A great dancer seeks to bring out the perfume and give the flower to her audience, rather than exhibit it in a glass case for them. Technique is a dancer's means of freeing her instrument so that it may carry the message of the dance; it is not the message itself.

A gifted artist invents her own movements from time to time to add to the basic repertoire of the dance. The only way of judging the correctness or otherwise of new movements is to consider whether or not they work, whether a dance in its entirety has unity and flow.

The same may be said of creating a costume

appropriate to tomorrow's dance. As an art, flamenco has had to overcome similar problems to those of Arabic dance. The difficulties are created by the commercialization of an art that is essentially best suited to small gatherings. Flamenco too was traditionally performed in everyday dress, but when it entered the commercial arena its costume altered less drastically than that of Arabic dance.

I recently saw a flamenco dancer wearing a brown blouse tucked into a plain skirt of a different shade of brown. She had no shawl, no flowers in her hair, no ornaments of any kind. Although she was performing against a black backdrop and I was sitting right at the back of the auditorium, her unadorned costume in no way prevented her from electrifying her audience. She had no tricks and little choreography; yet such was her artistry, such was the passion of her dancing, that the audience was held spellbound and when her dance was over, they erupted in a frenzy of appreciation.

In theatres a performer frequently finds herself working against a black backdrop. This makes certain demands on her costume simply in order to be seen. Yet it is not necessary to be covered in sequins to be visible from the back row; bright colours are equally successful. In developing a theatre art free of inappropriate associations, it may be necessary to avoid the type of costume which conjures up the commercial cabaret act (which requires its own particular skills and costuming). Nineteenth-century Arab dress, with its many-layered, multi-coloured skirts and shawls, its jewellery and elaborate hair coverings, may serve as the initial inspiration in the creation of a new costume for the dance. Whether or not this costume works depends on whether it is appropriate to the message a dancer is seeking to convey, or whether it conjures up an image which clashes with this message. This is especially true of the costume for *sharqi*, which is the form best suited to experimentation.

The current collaboration between Arab and Western musicians is paralleled by that of dancers experimenting with a fusion of disparate traditions by exploring the common elements of each. Certain artists are seeking to revive the vanished dances of the Middle East, such as the dance portrayed in the

Amel Benhassine-Miller in an Algerian bedouin dance. 1988. Photographs. Private collection

193

frescos of pharaonic Egypt, an enterprise which raises questions of authenticity and purity. We cannot say with any certainty what a dance which has not been seen for thousands of years looked like. In the final analysis we can only speculate, using the past as an inspiration to create dances based on the life of a former time. Purity and authenticity do not animate an entertainment; nor do they determine whether a piece works or not, or whether it gives pleasure to an audience.

Purity of form is a relative concept. This is especially true of *sharqi*, which has borrowed heavily not only from Asia and the West but also from the world of cabaret. *Sharqi* is the least pure of Arabic dance forms, and perhaps for this very reason is the one most open to innovation.

Artists attempting to define the solo dance in theatrical terms sometimes deny its origins, as well as its erotic element. They regard the latter as a particular source of embarrassment, something which will prevent the dance from ever achieving respectability in the arts. Meanwhile, government-sponsored troupes in the Arab world are compelled to play down this element in order to comply with the restrictions of their sponsors.

Leon Bakst. *Costume designs for 'Cleopatra' for the Ballets Russes.* Early 20th century. Watercolour. Private collection

The erotic element of Arabic dance has become its shadow side. This is unfortunate, for its exclusion strikes at the very root of *baladi* and *sharqi*. An element of eroticism can no more be excluded from Arabic dance than it can from, say, Western ballet. Art is a reflection of the human experience in its entirety. The fact that eroticism has acquired a negative connotation in most world cultures does not mean that it should be excluded from the arts. It demands, rather, a reappraisal.

In this context, it is interesting to consider the case of Indian dance. Over the past generation Indian dance has managed to redeem itself from the negative associations which paralleled those of Arabic dance. The two forms share similar roots and a notoriety acquired for much the same reasons. Western support was enlisted in the move to rehabilitate Indian dance, something which necessitated pandering to the puritanism of the West. As one writer on the subject has commented:

> Without the moral support of Western opinion, it is doubtful that young women of good family would have had the temerity to begin to study an ancient art so recently considered corrupt.[80]

Monika Kaiblinger. *Tunisian dancer.*
1986. Oil painting. Private collection

Indian culture is one of the few which celebrates sexual energy in the arts without a trace of negativity, welcoming it as an aspect of spiritual and transcendental experience. The drive towards a reassessment of Indian dance has been successful, yet at the cost of removing its more erotic aspects, to the extent that they are rarely mentioned in books on the subject, even in passing.

It would be unfortunate if such cultural censorship were to distort the future development of Arabic dance, which is at a crossroads in its history, with the misunderstanding which has hampered its development for so many years finally beginning to be dispelled.

Dancers from the Arab world who perform in the context of Western arts centres and festivals are often highly educated women who could have chosen a career other than the performing arts. In the past, it was extremely unusual for a woman from a highly placed Muslim family even to have considered entering the dance profession. Yet a growing number of women with this background, living in Europe and America, are now teaching and performing their dance here. They generally have to contend with considerable parental disapproval over their choice of a career. It takes a good deal of determination not to abandon their aim of making the dance respected among their own people, as well as pioneering its acceptance in the context of Western art.

A Tunisian dancer once said to me, 'If someone from my country asks me what I do for a living and I tell them I'm a dancer they say, "Mm. Very nice. But what do you do for a living?" ' This reply is an indication of how unusual it still is for a woman of her education to be an entertainer. It also reflects the degree to which, as she says herself, 'In my country, everyone's a dancer. Dancing's not work. You can't call it work. A day I don't dance is a day I don't live.'

Chapter 11

THE ESSENTIAL WOMAN

Could thou and I with fate conspire
To grasp this sorry scheme of things entire,
Would we not shatter it to bits,
And then remould it nearer to our heart's desire?

Omar Khayyam, *The Rubaiyat*

I recently watched a modern dance piece whose subject was 'today's woman', her feelings and sense of femininity. Two slim, crop-haired dancers in tee-shirts and baggy trousers circled each other tentatively, occasionally touching, then breaking free with a broad leap across the stage, arms grasping empty air. I must confess I found it rather a bleak manifestation of 'today's woman', if such a being exists. Its spare, angular movements, its absence of any joy, presented a dominant image of rejection of the body, distrust of a woman's sexuality rather than celebration.

Dance is shaped by the civilization in which it is found:

> [In the West] a love-hate relationship with the body colours all recent culture. The body is scorned and rejected as something inferior, and at the same time desired as something forbidden, objectified and alienated... In man's denigration of his own body, nature takes its revenge for the fact that man has reduced nature to an object for domination.[81]

These words, written forty years ago, are just as relevant today as they were then, despite our consistent attempts to come to terms with a religious and philosophical tradition which represses and devalues the body.

The 1960s was a time when attempts were made to transcend Western taboos and reassess the needs and desires of the human spirit. It is no accident that a driving force behind the youth culture of the period was provided by dance and music, nor that festivals, often described as 'tribal gatherings', were the most popular events of the decade. For music and dance are arts which bring people together like no other, and the sixties was a time of seeking to recreate a community spirit lost with the coming of industrialization and the decline of religious faith in the West.

It might be seen as a time which reflected Jung's belief that one of our great tasks is to reconcile the civilized and the primitive in us, to rediscover that lost intensity of living which can still be found in the rituals of remote communities. In our society today we have consciously to seek out this lost faith and ritual. We do this not only through the confessional of the psychiatrist's couch with the therapist as priest, but also through festivals of the performing arts.

The dance boom of the seventies and the growing interest in ethnic arts are a product of the sixties. At those gatherings and 'happenings' twenty years ago we danced with total abandon, as if casting off centuries of taboos against the pleasures of the senses. It was no longer necessary to have a partner, or even a partner of the opposite sex, nor to keep to a formal pattern of movement. Social dancing became wild and free, yet at the same time that it grew more abandoned it still remained the supreme expression of the individual — one has only to think of the isolated jogging about in a large group which has become our common mode of social dancing since then.

Individual self-expression without reference to others is a principal feature of Western dance today as a social activity. In the recent dance boom which has sent thousands of people, principally women, flocking to the studios, the most popular dances tend to be those which allow us to remain immersed in ourselves and our own isolated progress. They do not encourage us to appreciate other people's skills. Yet while solo dancing has its value, it is only one aspect of what dance has to offer us. Equally important is something we have lost in the West: a conscious union with others and an affirmation of them by means of dance.

Amel Benhassine-Miller has discovered that *baladi* and *sharqi* are more popular than the less demanding folk dance among her women students. She believes that people prefer the solo because it has most in common with the Western tradition in that, unlike bedouin dance, it does not require as great an interaction between people:

> Bedouin dance has a lot to do with the close nature of female relationships in the Arab world. This is something I miss in Europe. Women here don't have the same ease with themselves and each other's bodies as they do in my country.

It is true that women in the Arab world have a sensual ease and bodily awareness lacking in the West. Less hemmed in by external restrictions than in Arab countries, European and American women have, in a sense, created their own restrictions. These are manifested in a denial of the body and sensuality, as well as a physical stiffness and self-dislike from which Arab women in general do not suffer.

The feminist movement has never known quite how to address the question of female sensuality and until recently took refuge in near-androgyny as an inoffensive middle way. Yet many women find this image as oppressive as that of the glamour girl.

Stereotypes of female beauty are daily presented to us and reinforced by the media, in particular through advertising and film, which have taken over the female body for purposes of manipulation and titillation. Images of female beauty and desirability presented by these industries are based on slimness and eternal youth, stereotypes to which women have allowed themselves to become enslaved. Rather than accepting and caring for the body whatever its shape and size, and rather than accepting gracefully that we are all bound to grow old and that maturity has its advantages, many women allow themselves to be hoodwinked into pursuing goals which, even when achieved, do little to create self-confidence.

Arab ideals of beauty are more broadly based. One of the most rewarding sights at *baladi* dance classes in the West is to see the enjoyment of big-hipped, curvaceous women who have at last found a dance which allows them to take pride in their body, a dance in which they do not feel the odd one out.

Arabic dance is centred on self-expression,

sometimes alone, sometimes in relation to others. *Baladi* and *sharqi* allow us to explore the archetypes that are latent in all of us — archetypes of the coquette, the earth mother, the sensualist and the medium or poetess.

Over the past ten years or so, Arabic dance has attracted a growing following in the West. Today it is taught in towns and cities all over Europe and America, a phenomenon which has given rise to more media interest than it has enjoyed since the turn of the century. All too often the nature of this interest reflects long-held misapprehensions concerning the nature of the dance. When a woman expresses a desire to learn ethnic dance forms such as African, Indian or flamenco, it is not considered in any way newsworthy; yet when the subject is Arabic dance she is often greeted with raised eyebrows. The question most often asked is what Arabic dance offers Western women that is unique.

For every woman there is a different answer. One reason is that it is not an exclusive dance; no one is debarred from it by virtue of her age or physical size. Many women who would love to dance have been discouraged by the demands of Western dance forms such as ballet, whose requirements include a body of almost anorexic proportions. Classical ballet does little to question the predominant Western perception of the body as an encumbrance, something to be transcended rather than celebrated. It glorifies a kind of disembodied spirituality. Needless to say, it is difficult to compare two dance forms based on such a dissimilar aesthetic and use of the body. Yet by contrasting the two, we can understand something of the appeal of Arabic dance to modern sensibilities, and to women brought up with the balletic image as an ideal of feminine grace and beauty.

Interestingly, it is ballerinas who experience the greatest difficulty in learning Arabic dance, and they are often slow to come to terms with its images of women. For classical ballet is dedicated to woman as an ethereal being rather than a creature of flesh and blood. *Baladi*, in complete contrast, stresses woman's earthy qualities. *Sharqi*, while it has the fluid grace of ballet has, in addition, the rhythmic power of African dance and some of flamenco's passionate intensity.

Among the many attractions of Arabic dance is the chance to express the inner performer in all of us. Physical display is as much a part of the human experience as it is of the animal kingdom. Modern life offers us few opportunities to satisfy this need to display. Dressing up in rich colours, wearing jewellery and make-up is something many women love to do as much for their own self-respect as for the eyes of men, but they tend to feel out of place doing so in our increasingly informal society. Meanwhile, entertaining each other through bodily expression is almost unheard-of for most people, and after childhood is considered an unpardonable form of showing-off. To label someone an exhibitionist is to condemn them. Again we are confronted by the West's perception of the body as something inferior which needs to be played down, even apologized for. The performance element is vital in Arabic dance. To accept the need to get up in class and entertain the group, even if only for two or three minutes, is the greatest challenge of all for Western women; yet it is a challenge which, when met, goes a long way towards creating self-confidence.

Performing, even in an amateur capacity like this, confronts women with the ever-present, though unconscious, awareness that there is an ideal of female attractiveness and desirability to which they may not measure up. The Arabic dance tradition, with its acceptance of the body, whatever its shape, and its affirmation of a woman's sensuality, whatever her age, offers her the chance to reassess her own, sometimes negative self-image in an atmosphere of support rather than competition. Many women have found a sense of liberation in the dance's combination of the sensual and the poetic, its marriage of the earthy and the spiritual.

Arab women living in the West who have returned to the dance often comment on how it has helped them discover their identity in a strange country. As an Algerian friend of mine remarked, 'Living in Europe I became confused. I wasn't dancing then. I was working as a translator. I began asking myself, what is my identity? Was I European? Was I Arab? It is through the dance that I have been able to define myself as a woman.' Many Western women who are drawn to Arabic dance cannot say exactly

201

where the attraction lies. Initially, all they know is that it fascinates them; only later do they discover that, through dancing, they have come to explore aspects of their essential femininity with which they had lost touch.

My own most valued experiences of the dance have come when performing at social gatherings among Arab families. In this situation the dance has frequently been illumined for me as a tradition whose significance is as alive today as it was thousands of years ago. I once danced at the London wedding of a Yemeni girl whose friends and relatives had flown in specially for the occasion. For convenience, the reception was held at a hotel attached to the airport. After the formal entertainment was over a man appeared with a mobile disco for the young people. In the early hours of the morning the guests began drifting back to their hotel rooms, and the bride's father told us he wanted us to send the bride and groom on their way in the old style. This meant taking them from the party with singing and drumming and finger cymballing, with the guests joining in the procession.

And so we set out across the cavernous foyer, empty at that early hour save for a handful of hotel staff manning the reception desk. We made our way to the lift accompanied by the young girls from the party, resplendent in designer dresses, trailing clouds of French perfume. They crowded round the bride and groom, their hands raised above their heads, rhythmically clapping and singing and jostling each other in their excitement, with the older women and a few of the men bringing up the rear.

After the lift doors had swung smoothly shut on the smiling pair, the girls continued with their singing and hand-clapping. It was obvious that they were enjoying themselves far more now than they had done over their desultory disco dancing earlier on. Everyone was reluctant to leave and hovered about in the foyer in the vain hope that this new party might somehow be prolonged indefinitely. There, in the grand, cold setting of an air-conditioned hotel with the sound of jets arriving and departing just outside the door, a tradition which has survived from the ancient world asserted its value once again in the face of a more sophisticated age.

Notes

Introduction

1. Juvenal, *Satire*, from *Juvenal and Persius*, transl. G.G. Ramsay (Putnam's, New York, 1924), vol. ix, lines 162ff, pp. 232ff.

2. Mas'udi, *Meadows of Gold and Mines of Gems*, transl. C. Barbier de Meynard (Société Asiatique, Paris, 1874), vol. viii, p. 100.

3. Charles Gobineau, *The Dancing Girl of Shamahka and Other Asiatic Tales* (Cape, London, 1926), p. 43.

4. G.W. Curtis, *Nile Notes of a Howadji* (Vizetelly, London, 1852), p. 88.

5. Ibid.

Chapter 1

6. Mircea Eliade, *Myths, Dreams and Mysteries* (Fontana, London, 1970), p. 219.

7. Margaret Mead, *Male and Female* (Morrow, New York, 1949), p. 98.

8. Curt Sachs, *World History of the Dance* (Allen & Unwin, London, 1938), p. 47.

9. Joseph Spurrier, as quoted in Cherry Hopkins, *The Hula* (Apa Productions, Hong Kong, 1982), p. 32.

10. Lillian B. Lawler, 'Terpsichore: The Story of Dance in Ancient Greece', *Dance Perspectives Magazine*, New York, winter 1962, pp. 47ff.

11. For a discussion of matriarchal culture and anthropological/archeological indications of its existence in prehistoric times, see Elizabeth Gould Davis, *The First Sex* (Penguin, Harmondsworth, 1972) and Merlin Stone, *The Paradise Papers* (Virago, London, 1979).

12. Eliade, *Myths, Dreams and Mysteries*, p. 156.

13. Hesiod, as quoted in Nancy Qualls-Corbett, *The Sacred Prostitute* (Inner City Books, Toronto, 1988), p. 34.

14. Clifford Howard, *Sex Worship* (Clifford Howard, Washington DC, 1897), p. 93.

15. Theodor Reik, *Pagan Rites in Judaism* (Farrar, New York, 1964), p. 100.

16. W.R. Smith, as quoted in ibid., p. 70. For a discussion of the prevalence of the goddess religion in the ancient world, see Gould Davis, *First Sex*.

17. James Frazer, *The Golden Bough* (Macmillan, London, 1971), p. 460.

Chapter 2

18. Macrobius, as quoted in Otto Kiefer, *Sexual Life in Ancient Rome* (Barnes & Noble, New York, 1934), p. 167.

19. W.L. Westermann, 'The Castanet Dancers of Arsinoe', *Journal of Egyptian Archeology*, London, 1924, p. 135.

20. Rev. James Neil, *Everyday Life in the Holy Land* (Cassell, London, 1913), p. 77.

21. As quoted in Sarah Graham-Brown, *Images of Women* (Quartet, London, 1988), p. 128.

22. Lucie Duff Gordon, *Letters from Egypt* (Virago, London, 1983), p. 20.

23. Huda Shaarawi, *Harem Years* (Virago, London, 1986), p. 42.

Chapter 3

24. Edward Said, *Orientalism* (Routledge & Kegan Paul, London, 1978).

25. Eugène Delacroix, as quoted in Philippe Jullian, *The Orientalists* (Phaidon, Oxford, 1977), p. 48.

26. Carsten Niebuhr, *Travels Through Arabia* (no pub., Edinburgh, 1790), p. 153.

27. Charles Leland, *The Egyptian Sketchbook* (Strahan, London, 1873), p. 126.

28. Charles Didier, *Les Nuits de Caire*, transl. Bernice Terluin (Hachette, Paris, 1860), p. 329.

29. James Augustus St John, *Egypt and Nubia: Their Scenery and Their People* (Chapman & Hall, London, 1845), p. 274.

30. Charles Frédéric Alexandre de Carcy, *De Paris en Egypte, Souvenirs de Voyage* (Berger-Levrault, Paris, 1874), p. 236.

31. Leland, *Egyptian Sketchbook*, p. 126.

32. E.W. Lane, *The Modern Egyptians* (Charles Knight, London, 1846), vol. 2, p. 225.

33. Leland, *Egyptian Sketchbook*, p. 128.

34. Charles Blanc, *Voyage de la Haute Egypte; Observations sur les Arts Egyptiens et Arabes* (Renouard, Paris, 1876), p. 50.

35. Rev. James Neil, *Everyday Life in the Holy Land* (Cassell, London, 1913), p. 197.

36. Lucie Duff Gordon, *Letters from Egypt* (Virago, London, 1983), p. 100.

37. Gerard de Nerval, *The Women of Cairo* (Routledge, London, 1929), p. 65.

38. Duff Gordon, *Letters from Egypt*, p. 100.

39. Leland, *Egyptian Sketchbook*, p. 132.

40. Didier, *Nuits de Caire*, p. 330.

41. G.W. Curtis, *Nile Notes of a Howadji* (Vizetelly, London, 1852), p. 88.

42. Maxime du Camp, as quoted in Francis Steegmuller, *Flaubert in Egypt* (Academy, Chicago, 1979), p. 154.

43. Ibid., p. 214.

Notes

Chapter 4

44. Hector de Callias, as quoted in 'Western Art and its Encounter with the Islamic World' in Mary Anne Stevens, *The Orientalists* (Royal Academy of Arts, London, 1984), p.20.

45. For a discussion of the history of women's social position under Islam, see Fatima Mernissi, *Beyond the Veil* (Al Saqi, London, 1985).

46. Lady Mary Wortley Montagu, *Travel Letters* (Jonathan Cape, London, 1930), p.155.

47. Rana Kabbani, *Europe's Myths of Orient* (Pandora, London, 1986), p.69.

48. Ted Shawn, *Gods Who Dance* (Dutton, New York, 1929), p.182.

49. Ibid.

50. Colette, *Places* (Peter Owen, London, 1970), pp.79ff.

51. Ibid.

Chapter 5

52. *The Illustrated American*, Chicago, Nov. 1893.

53. Bernard Sobel, *Burleycue: An Underground History of Burlesque Days* (Farrar & Rinehart, New York, 1931), p.63.

54. *The Illustrated American*, Chicago, Nov. 1893.

55. Armen Ohanian, *Les Rires d'une Charmeuse de Serpents* (Les Revues, Paris, 1931), p.30.

56. Armen Ohanian, *The Dancer of Shamahka* (Jonathan Cape, London, 1922), pp.176ff.

57. Ibid., p.247.

58. Ibid., p.260.

59. Ohanian, *Rires d'une Charmeuse*, pp.148ff.

60. Ibid., p.153.

61. Ohanian, *Dancer of Shamahka*, p.246.

Chapter 6

62. Peter Leslie, *A Hard Act To Follow — A Music Hall Review* (Paddington, London, 1978), p.53.

63. Bernard Sobel, *Burleycue: An Underground History of Burlesque Days* (Farrar & Rinehart, New York, 1931), p.104.

64. Ruth St Denis, *An Unfinished Life* (Harrap, London, 1939), p.96.

65. Ibid., p.97.

66. Colette, *My Apprenticeships and Music Hall Sidelights* (Penguin, Harmondsworth, 1967), p.16.

67. Colette, *The Vagabond* (Penguin, Harmondsworth, 1960), p.38.

68. Colette, *My Apprenticeships*, p.180.

69. Margaret Crosland, *Colette; The Difficulty of Loving* (Dell, New York, 1973), p.104.

70. Julia Keay, *The Spy Who Never Was* (Michael Joseph, London, 1988), p.35.

71. J.K. Huysmans, *Against Nature* (Penguin, Harmondsworth, 1959), p.65.

72. Hugo von Hoffmannsthal, as quoted in Walter Sorell, *Dance in its Time* (Anchor Press, Doubleday, New York, 1981), p.337.

73. Gustave Flaubert, 'Herodias' from *Three Tales* (Penguin, Harmondsworth, 1961), p.120.

Chapter 7

74. Morroe Berger, 'The Arab Danse du Ventre', *Dance Perspectives Magazine*, New York, spring 1961.

Chapter 8

75. Bimbashi McPherson, *The Man Who Loved Egypt* (Airel Books, BBC, London, 1985), p.226.

76. Ibid., p.228.

77. S. Deaver, 'Concealment Versus Display; The Modern Saudi', as quoted in *Arabesque Magazine*, New York, vol.x, no.1 (May/June 1984), p.34.

Chapter 9

78. Laurel Victoria Gray, 'Music and Dance within the Islamic Context', *Arabesque Magazine*, New York, vol.x, no.1 (May/June 1984), p.34.

79. Charles Frédéric Alexandre de Carcy, *De Paris en Egypte, Souvenirs de Voyage* (Berger-Levrault, Paris, 1874).

Chapter 10

80. Leona Wood, 'Nautchees and Devadasis', *Arabesque Magazine*, New York, vol.xiv, no.1 (May/June 1988), p.12.

Chapter 11

81. Max Horkheimer and Theodor Adorno, 'Dialectic of Enlightenment', as quoted in Jonathan Benthall, *The Body Electric: Patterns of Western Industrial Culture* (Thames & Hudson, London, 1976), p.71.

Select Bibliography

Bachofen, J.J. *Myth, Religion and Mother Rite* (Princeton University Press, Princeton, 1967)

Bancroft, Hubert Howe. *The Book of the Fair* (Bancroft, Chicago, 1895)

Berque, Jacques. *Egypt: Imperialism and Revolution* (Faber, London, 1972)

Boudhiba, A. *Islam and Sexuality* (Routledge & Kegan Paul, London, 1985)

Briffault, Robert. *The Mothers* (Grosset & Dunlop, New York, 1963)

Buchner, A. *Folk Instruments of the World* (Crown, New York, 1972)

Bulos, A. Alvarez. *Handbook of Arabic Music* (Librairie du Liban, Beirut, 1971)

Buschow, R. *The Prince and I* (Futura, London, 1979)

Campbell, Joseph. *The Hero With A Thousand Faces* (Princeton University Press, Princeton, 1949)

Colette. *The Vagabond* (Penguin, Harmondsworth, 1960)

Curtis, G.W. *Nile Notes of a Howadji* (Vizetelly, London, 1852)

Duff Gordon, Lucie. *Letters from Egypt* (Virago, London, 1983)

Eliade, Mircea. *Myths, Dreams and Mysteries* (Fontana, London, 1970)

Ellis, Havelock. *The Dance of Life* (Houghton Mifflin, New York, 1923)

Fernea, E.W. *Guests of the Sheik* (Anchor Press, Doubleday, New York, 1969)

—— *A Street in Marrakesh* (Anchor Press, Doubleday, New York, 1976)

Flaubert, Gustave. *Three Tales* (Penguin, Harmondsworth, 1961)

Frazer, James. *The Golden Bough: A Study in Magic and Religion* (Macmillan, London, 1971)

Gould Davis, Elizabeth. *The First Sex* (Penguin, New York, 1971)

Graham-Brown, Sarah. *Images of Women* (Quartet, London, 1988)

Guest, Ivor. *The Ballet of the Second Empire* (Black, London, 1955)

—— *Victorian Ballet Girls* (Black, London, 1957)

Kendall, E. *Where She Danced* (Knopf, New York, 1979)

Lane, E.W. *The Modern Egyptians* (Charles Knight, London, 1864)

Lewis, Bernard. *The Arabs in History* (Harper & Row, New York, 1966)

Mead, Margaret. *Male and Female* (Morrow, New York, 1949)

Mernissi, Fatima. *Beyond the Veil. Male-Female Dynamics in Modern Muslim Society* (Al Saqi, London, 1985)

Parker, D. & J. *The Natural History of the Chorus Girl* (David & Charles, Newton Abbot, 1975)

Pohren, D.E. *The Art of Flamenco* (Musical New Services, Dorset, 1984)

Saadawi, Nawal El. *The Hidden Face of Eve* (Zed, London, 1980)

Sachs, Curt. *World History of the Dance* (Allen & Unwin, London, 1938)

Said, Edward. *Orientalism* (Routledge & Kegan Paul, London, 1978)

Shaarawi, Huda. *Harem Years* (Virago, London, 1986)

Shawn, Ted. *Gods Who Dance* (Dutton, New York, 1929)

Sorell, Walter. *Dance in its Time* (Anchor Press, Doubleday, New York, 1981)

Steegmuller, Francis. *Flaubert In Egypt; A Sensibility on Tour* (Academy, Chicago, 1979)

Stone, Merlin. *The Paradise Papers* (Virago, London, 1976)

Thomas, Keith. *Religion and the Decline of Magic* (Penguin, Harmondsworth, 1971)

Webb, Peter. *The Erotic Arts* (Secker & Warburg, London, 1983)

Index

Index